M000169730

QUICK AND EASY
Jigs AND Fixtures

KERRY PIERCE

POPULAR WOODWORKING BOOKS
CINCINNATI, OHIO
www.popularwoodworking.com

READ THIS IMPORTANT SAFETY NOTICE

To prevent accidents, keep safety in mind while you work. Use the safety guards installed on power equipment; they are for your protection. When working on power equipment, keep fingers away from saw blades, wear safety goggles to prevent injuries from flying wood chips and sawdust, wear headphones to protect your hearing, and consider installing a dust vacuum to reduce the amount of airborne sawdust in your woodshop. Don't wear loose clothing, such as neckties or shirts with loose sleeves, or jewelry, such as rings, necklaces or bracelets, when working on power equipment. Tie back long hair to prevent it from getting caught in your equipment. People who are sensitive to certain chemicals should check the chemical content of any product before using it. The authors and editors who compiled this book have tried to make the contents as accurate and correct as possible. Plans, illustrations, photographs and text have been carefully checked. All instructions, plans and projects should be carefully read, studied and understood before beginning construction. In some photos, power tool guards have been removed to more clearly show the operation being demonstrated. Always use all safety guards and attachments that come with your power tools. Due to the variability of local conditions, construction materials, skill levels, etc., neither the author nor Popular Woodworking Books assumes any responsibility for any accidents, injuries, damages or other losses incurred resulting from the material presented in this book. Prices listed for supplies and equipment were current at the time of publication and are subject to change. Glass shelving should have all edges polished and must be tempered. Untempered glass shelves may shatter and can cause serious bodily injury. Tempered shelves are very strong and if they break will just crumble, minimizing personal injury.

Quick and Easy Jigs and Fixtures. Copyright © 2005 by Kerry Pierce. Printed and bound in China. All rights reserved. No part of this book may be reproduced in any form or by any electronic or mechanical means including information storage and retrieval systems without permission in writing from the publisher, except by a reviewer, who may quote brief passages in a review. Published by Popular Woodworking Books, an imprint of F+W Publications, Inc., 4700 East Galbraith Road, Cincinnati, Ohio, 45236. First edition.

Distributed in Canada by Fraser Direct
100 Armstrong Avenue
Georgetown, Ontario L7G 5S4
Canada

Distributed in the U.K. and Europe by David & Charles
Brunel House
Newton Abbot
Devon TQ12 4PU
England
Tel: (+44) 1626 323200
Fax: (+44) 1626 323319
E-mail: mail@davidandcharles.co.uk

Distributed in Australia by Capricorn Link
P.O. Box 704
Windsor, NSW 2756
Australia

Visit our Web site at www.popularwoodworking.com for information on more resources for woodworkers.

Other fine Popular Woodworking Books are available from your local bookstore or direct from the publisher.

09 08 07 06 05   5 4 3 2 1

Library of Congress Cataloging-in-Publication Data

Pierce, Kerry.
    Quick and easy jigs and fixtures / Kerry Pierce. -- 1st ed.
        p.   cm.
    Includes index.
    ISBN 1-55870-709-3 (pbk. : alk. paper), 1-55870-765-4 (hardcover: alk. paper)
    1. Chairs.   2. Furniture making.   I. Title.
TT197.5.C45P56   2005
684'.08--dc22   2005000215

ACQUISITIONS EDITOR: Jim Stack
EDITOR: Amy Hattersley
DESIGNER: Brian Roeth
COVER AND CHAPTER OPENER PHOTOGRAPHY BY:
    Tim Grondin
PRODUCTION COORDINATOR: Jennifer Wagner
MEASURED DRAWINGS BY: Kevin Pierce

fw
F+W PUBLICATIONS, INC.

About the Author

For over a quarter century, Kerry Pierce has specialized in post-and-rung chairmaking. He is the author of over ten woodworking books, including *The Art of Chair-Making, Making Elegant Gifts from Wood, The Custom Furniture Sourcebook* and *Authentic Shaker Furniture*. Since 1995, he's served as contributing editor of *Woodwork* and is a frequent contributor to that magazine. His chairs have been exhibited at a number of Ohio venues, most recently at "Ohio Furniture by Contemporary Masters" at the Ohio Decorative Arts Center. He has also been a chairmaking instructor at the Marc Adams School of Woodworking.

Acknowledgements

In October of 2003, I was diagnosed with Stage 4, non-Hodgkins lymphoma. I was given only a slight chance of surviving the disease. At the time of my diagnosis, I had just begun work on this book, so shortly after I received the bad news, I contacted my editor at Popular Woodworking Books, Jim Stack, and explained I would be unable to finish the book by the June 2004 deadline stipulated in our contract. In fact, I said, I might not be able to finish it at all. Then I put the book aside and concentrated on my illness.

For the next six months, I fought my cancer with a series of intense, five-day-long chemotherapy sessions. The chemo was potent stuff, so potent, in fact, that the nurses who loaded my IV double-gloved their hands before touching the bags in which the toxins were stored.

My response to chemotherapy was better than my doctors had expected, and after six months, my cancer was in remission. The war wasn't over, but I had won the first battle. In March, when my oncologist gave me the green light to return to the shop — although on a limited basis — I e-mailed Jim Stack to see if they had any work I could do to earn the advance money they'd already paid me for this jig-and-fixture book, money which I'd already spent on medical bills.

He said: "Sure. Why not finish the book?"

That, I think, says a lot about the kind of people I work for at Popular Woodworking Books. I had assumed that this book had been assigned to someone else during the months I was out of commission. After all, my failure to deliver on time had left a hole in the company's publication schedule. But they didn't give the book to someone else. Instead, they shuffled things around to fill in the gap in their publication schedule and held onto this title until I was ready to go back to work on it.

Maybe it wasn't a smart business decision, but it was the only decision the people at Pop Wood were capable of making.

So thanks, Jim, and everybody else at Pop Wood who had a hand in treating me so well during my illness.

Thanks to John LaVine at *Woodwork* magazine, who, when he realized I could no longer work in the shop, offered me writing assignments that didn't require me to get dusty.

Thanks also to Roger Mace and Martie Moore who endeavored to keep my shop remodel moving forward when I was on the physically-unable-to-perform list.

Thanks also to Dr. Porcu and the staff at The James Cancer Hospital in Columbus, Ohio, for their gracious handling of a sometimes cranky cancer patient.

And thanks, also, to my wife, Elaine; my daughter, Emily; my son, Andy; my parents Jim and Sally; my brother, Kevin; my friend, Verne; and everybody else who stood with me during a long and difficult year.

TABLE OF CONTENTS

INTRODUCTION

I started this book with the intention of writing yet another volume about jigs and fixtures, a topic which is understandably attractive to woodworkers. Jigs and fixtures, after all, make woodworking so much easier and so much more pleasurable by making it possible to get good results the first time out and every time thereafter.

But halfway through my work on the book, I realized that what I wanted to do was something a little different. Instead of writing about jigs and fixtures only, I wanted to write about how work is conducted in the presence of shop-made work aides, including — but not limited to — the jigs and fixtures I originally set out to describe.

I think this approach occurred to me because at the same time I was working on this book, I was also working on the first big remodel my shop had seen in almost twenty years. That remodel included the construction of a very sizable wood rack which permitted me — for the first time — to gain the upper hand in my thirty-year battle with scrap. It also included new cabinets for my radial arm saw's infeed and outfeed tables, new paint, new lighting, new air conditioning, over 80 lineal feet of new shelf space, and a new wheeled stand for my planer, which allows me to roll this particularly dirty machine to the door of my shop so that it ejects its Amazonian stream of shavings into the driveway instead of onto the floor of my shop.

Therefore, with the kind indulgence of Jim Stack, my editor at Popular Woodworking Books, I've included a chapter on shop design, along with photos and drawings of some of the constructions I've built to help me make better use of my woodworking time and efforts.

WOOD STORAGE RACK
FRONT VIEW

$3\frac{1}{2}$

PORTABLE
PLANER

JOINTER

TABLE SAW

CHAPTER ONE

Drawing Aides

Good woodworking begins with good layout work. As you know, no matter how skillful you are with your woodworking tools, you can't find success in the shop unless you've also found success doing the preliminary work of laying out each new piece.

Some of the ideas contained in this chapter deal specifically with the issue of drawing; for example, the beam compass and the bent stick for creating curved lines. But the most important feature of this chapter is, I think, the section on story sticks.

Much of the work I do in my shop requires me to repeat, with some modest variations, pieces I've made many times before. For example, I probably make 10 or 15 Shaker no.5 side chairs each year. Without the clutch of story sticks I have hanging from the wall of my shop, I would have to open my folding rule 19 times to measure the length of each of an individual chair's 19 wood parts. And I would have to repeat those 19 measurements for each of the 10 or 15 chairs I build each year. Yet, because of my story sticks, I'm able to keep that folding rule in my hip pocket where it belongs.

Angle Marking Gauge (Bevel Square)

Chairmaking accounts for most of the work produced in my shop, and when I'm adding a new chair to my repertoire, I first prepare a measured drawing. One of the key elements in that drawing is an accurate representation from above of the angles at which the side rungs and the front rungs meet, as well as the angles at which the side rungs and the back rungs meet.

A factory-made bevel gauge just doesn't have the reach to provide the necessary accuracy. This shop-built, long-legged gauge, however, does have the reach.

STEP 1 After ripping out and thicknessing the cherry from which you'll cut the two arms of your gauge, round one end of the stock from which you will later cut the tongued arm.

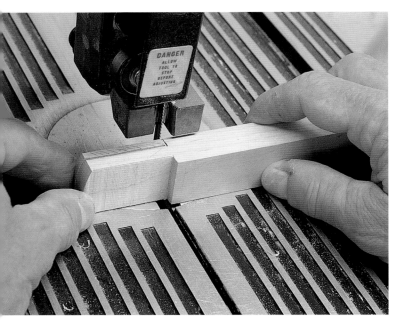

STEP 2 Then, after cleaning up the saw marks on the rounded end, turn the piece on its edge and cut the tongue to the proper thickness.

STEP 3 With the stock clamped to your bench top, use a butt chisel as a scraper to clean up the tool marks on each face of the tongue.

STEP **4** Then, on the other arm, mark the notch into which the tongue will be fit. When you're cutting this notch, keep the blade of your bandsaw on the waste side of the pencil line. Then clean up the interior faces of the notch with a rasp and file.

STEP **5** The two legs of the gauge are held together with a brass bolt. To drill the hole through which the bolt would pass, tape the legs, in the proper alignment, to a bit of scrap. Then drill the hole on your drill press.

STEP **6** The arms of this gauge are long enough to give you accurate measurements of chair seat angles.

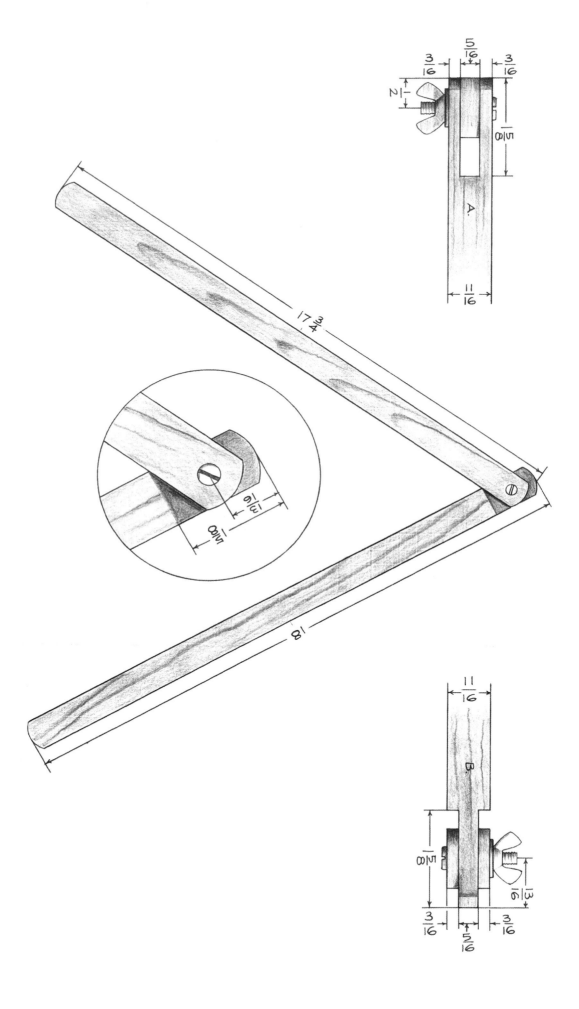

INCHES (MILLIMETERS)

REFERENCE	QUANTITY	PART	STOCK	THICKNESS	(mm)	WIDTH	(mm)	LENGTH	(mm)
A	1	notched arm		11/16	(18)	1	(25)	17 3/4	(451)
B	1	tongued arm		11/16	(18)	1	(25)	18	(457)

Beam Compass

The legs on the little metal compass I keep in my marking tool drawer will only extend to a bit less than 6", which limits the circles I can draw with this device to approximately 11 1/2". Also, when the legs are extended to near maximum length, the angles at which the compass' centerpoint and pencil meet the work surface are so extreme that it's hard to render accurate circles.

Recently, I found myself making a number of round tabletops, all of which measured 12+ inches. To draw the top for the first of these, I made a single-use compass by drilling a pencil-sized hole in one end of a length of scrap and driving a nail through the other end. This device enabled me to draw circles with a radius equal to the distance between the pencil point and the tip of the nail. It was not, however, adjustable, and when I found myself faced with the construction of a pair of tabletops with a different diameter, I decided to make an adjustable beam compass, one that would allow me to draw circles with a diameter of between 5" (anything less is within the grasp of my metal compass) and 47", which is a greater diameter than any round tabletop I've ever made.

STEP **1** Begin by cutting out the head stock (the part that will hold the pencil with which you will render circles). Because I so often work in cherry and therefore have so much cherry scrap on hand, I chose cherry for the compass' head and tail stocks. The head and tail stock were both band-sawn in two adjacent planes, much like the process of creating cabriole legs for period furniture. Sketch the necessary shapes on one side of a cherry block, then go to the bandsaw and begin cutting. Notice the many relief cuts. These make it possible to follow the relatively tight radii on the compass parts.

STEP **2** With a rasp, clean up tool marks.

STEP 3 Sketch the head stock shape on the adjacent plane. I chose to do this freehand because this method of work recognizes that the object's overall visual appeal is more important than symmetry. Plus, most of the surfaces of this part don't have to mate with surfaces on any other part, which relieves me of the obligation to create precisely uniform surfaces.

STEP 4 After making relief cuts, saw out this adjacent plane.

STEP 5 Clean up the tool marks. Then locate the center of the hole into which the marking pencil will be fit. An awl mark will help to align the center point of the drill bit.

STEP **6** Drill the pencil hole on the drill press. Pencils come in many different diameters. Bore some test holes in scrap to make sure that you have a bit that is the same size as the pencil you've chosen. You want the pencil to fit into the hole freely but without slop.

STEP **7** Next, drill the hole into which you will turn the ¾" no.6 brass wood screw that will hold the pencil in place. Drill bit size is critical, particularly when you're turning brass screws into a hardwood like cherry because it's very easy to twist brass screws to the breaking point. Unfortunately, there is no table to which you can turn when selecting drill bit size for such an application. The only way to determine the correct size bit is through experimentation. Drill a couple holes that look approximately right in a piece of scrap. Then, turn the screw into the holes. You want a hole that is small enough for the threads to engage the walls without being so small that the screw twists off. (Some woodworkers first turn a steel screw of the same size and pitch into the hole, and while this idea makes good sense, I never seem to have steel screws of the same specifications as the brass screws I'm intending to use.)

STEP **8** For aesthetic reasons, I decided to fit the ends of the beams into shallow mortises in the head stock. Begin the mortises by outlining them with carving gouges of the appropriate radii.

STEP 9 Then, lever the chips out with a paring chisel.

STEP 10 Next, cut out the tail stock, again band-sawing the blank in two adjacent planes.

STEP 11 A 10-24 x ½" brass machine screw turned into a 10-24 brass wood-insert nut locks the tail stock into position along the dual beams of this compass. After cleaning up band saw marks on the tail stock, turn the wood-insert nut into a pre-drilled hole using a screwdriver fixed in the slot cut in the top of the wood-insert nut, as shown here. (Notice the extra wood-insert nut to the right of the screwdriver tip.) Here, too, I had to be careful with hole size. Too large a hole and the threads on the outside of the wood-insert nut wouldn't engage. Too small a hole and the screwdriver would break apart the top of the wood-insert nut. As always, buy extra hardware and experiment with hole sizes in scrap.

STEP 12 This photo shows the machine screw that will be turned into the wood-insert nut.

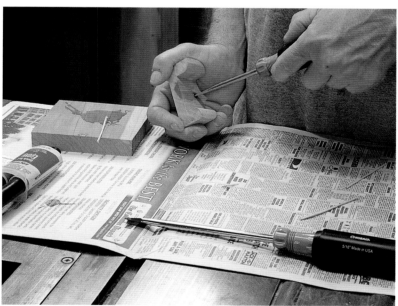

STEP 13 Because the wood-insert nut didn't tighten up sufficiently in the hole (I had to drill the hole a bit too large to keep the brass fitting from breaking apart when I turned it in), I mixed up some two-part epoxy, coated the nut with the mixture, and re-installed the nut in the tail stock.

STEP 14 I chose hard maple for the dual beams, both because it offered a nice color contrast to the cherry of the head and tail stock, and because it is strong, even when dressed to a thickness of less than $\frac{1}{4}$". For aesthetic reasons, I countersunk the heads of the no.6 x $\frac{3}{8}$" brass wood screws that hold the dual beams to the head stock.

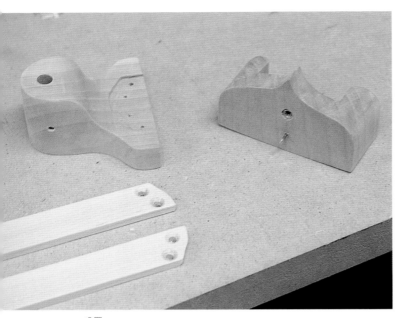

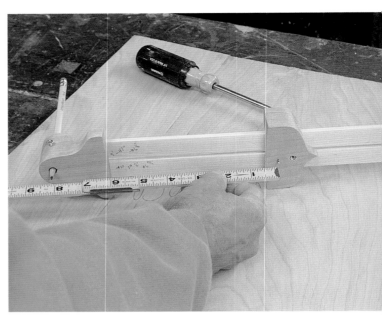

STEP 15 These parts have been sanded and are ready to be assembled. Notice the centerpoint protruding from the bottom of the tail stock. This is nothing but a sharpened 4d nail from which I'd cut the head tapped into a hole drilled in the underside of the tail stock.

STEP 16 To prepare the beam compass for use, set the tail stock so the distance from the center point to the pencil point is exactly half the diameter of the circle you're going to draw. Then, lock the tail stock into position by tightening the machine screw in the wood-insert nut. In this photo, I've set the compass to draw a circle 16¼" in diameter.

STEP 17 To draw a circle, place the tail stock's centerpoint at the center of the circle and, holding it in place with gentle pressure from one hand, use the other hand to rotate the head stock around that centerpoint.

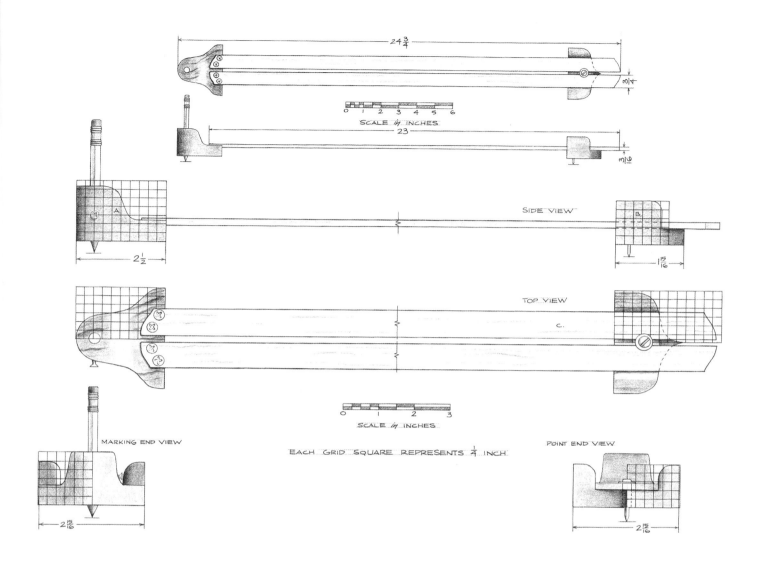

SCALE IN INCHES

SIDE VIEW

TOP VIEW

MARKING END VIEW

POINT END VIEW

SCALE in INCHES

EACH GRID SQUARE REPRESENTS 1/4 INCH

INCHES (MILLIMETERS)

REFERENCE	QUANTITY	PART	STOCK	THICKNESS	(mm)	WIDTH	(mm)	LENGTH	(mm)
A	1	head stock		$1^5/8$	(41)	$2^1/2$	(64)	$2^{15}/16$	(75)
B	1	tail stock		$1^1/4$	(32)	$1^{15}/16$	(49)	$2^{15}/16$	(75)
C	2	beams		$3/16$	(5)	$3/4$	(19)	23	(584)

HARDWARE & SUPPLIES

$1^3/4$" (19mm) #6 set screw

$4^3/8$" (10mm) #6 wood screws

110" x 24" (254mm x 610mm) wood insert nut

Strips of Wood for Drawing Curves

With the help of an assistant, in this case my son, Andy, you can draw attractive curves along a sprung piece of thin hardwood. In this photo, I'm holding a thin strip of knot-free hard maple so that it touches three measured points on the glued up panel: one at either end and one in the middle. While I'm holding it, Andy is drawing a line along one side.

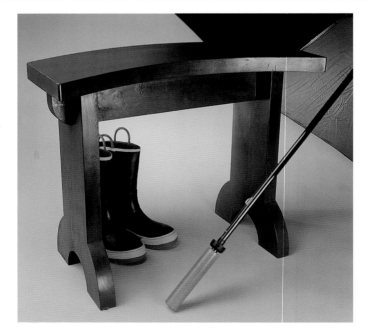

This is the bench, the top of which Andy is drawing in the previous photo.

Story Sticks

Each of the chairs I build in my shop is represented by a set of story sticks hanging on the wall beside my lathe. All the information I need to build each of these chairs is written on these sticks: length of parts, mortise placement, even the required turned shapes.

This photo shows the group of story sticks hanging beside my lathe.

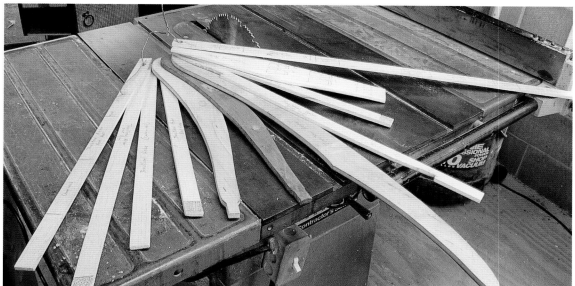

This particular array of sticks represents a Shaker transitional rocker, one of the most popular chairs in my line. In addition to slat and rocker patterns, this array includes two different arm shapes.

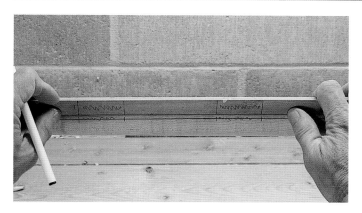

In these photos, I'm transferring mortise placement information from the story stick to a chair post.

21

CHAPTER TWO

Table-saw Aides

I don't do a lot of table-saw-based work in my shop. I spend much more time at the band saw and at the lathe, but I have designed several simple table-saw jigs that allow me to more efficiently cut wide panels to length, to create raised panels with a hollow-ground planer blade, and to quickly form tenons on the ends of curved table legs.

Of these three jigs, my favorite is the cutoff box. While mine borrows extensively from the million other cutoff boxes out there, mine has one nifty feature I can't recall having seen on any other cutoff box — a turned vertical handle rising up out of the box exactly where you want it when you reach out with your right hand.

Cutoff Box (Sled)

If you don't have a radial-arm saw and you want to cut material accurately to length, a table-saw cutoff box might be what you need. Not only will it allow you to make these cuts quickly and efficiently, it will — if you're careful enough with your construction work — produce a 90° angle every time, something few radial-arm saw setups can promise.

And even if you have a radial-arm saw, you may find the cutoff box a necessary tool because it will allow you to cross cut material 18", 20", even 24" wide. This is something you can't do on your radial arm saw unless you cut halfway, flip the material and cut halfway again.

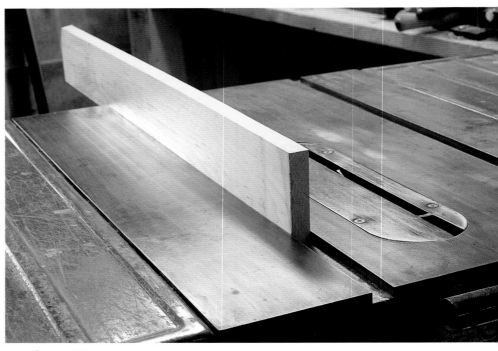

STEP 1 The cutoff box runs on a pair of hardwood strips fit into your table saw's miter-gauge slots. Begin work on your cutoff box by thicknessing a piece of hard maple (or another similarly durable wood) until it fits comfortably in the slots, moving freely back and forth without any slop.

STEP 2 I used to use Baltic birch for jigs and fixtures. It has the advantage of voidless internal laminations which offer a bit more strength and rigidity. Yet, I've found that if I sort through the birch plywood at my local Lowe's, I can usually find something that is flat enough and sound enough for almost any jig construction and at a much cheaper price than I would pay for Baltic birch.

I wouldn't recommend fir plywood. Yes, it is even cheaper than conventional birch plywood, but it is rarely flat, and it is almost impossible to flatten unless you're nailing it to the side of a building, and jigs need to be made of material that is as close to flat as possible.

I decided on a box with a 22" cutting capacity. I have one even wider, but it's a little cumbersome to use. This time I decided to go with the widest box I could make from a 24" x 48" piece of birch plywood, one of the standard sizes offered by Lowe's.

In this photo, I'm marking the locations of the two hardwood strips on which the box will ride.

STEP 3 Square a line back from each of these marks. This squaring procedure is very important. If you don't take the time to do this carefully, your cutoff box will never make 90° cuts. In this photo, I'm marking lines on the underside of the plywood, the side to which my hardwood miter gauge strips will be screwed.

(I know: My framing square is a mess. I've had it for thirty years, using it on innumerable indoor and outdoor jobs. The result is that it's rusted and pitted and covered with paint. But, its legs are still an exact 90° apart.)

STEP 4 Screw the maple strips to the underside of the sheet of plywood using a bunch of 1" no.8 Phillips wood screws, carefully aligning the sides of the strips with the lines you drew, as shown in the previous photo. The heads of these screws must be recessed so they don't catch in the miter gauge slot.

STEP 5 I then tested the box pressing the maple strips in the miter gauge slots. As expected, the fit was a little too snug. This snugness isn't a result of strips which are too wide. It is, almost certainly, a result of strips which are not perfectly aligned with the pencil lines. To correct the problem, I used a butt chisel as a scraper and pared off thin shavings from the sides of the strips.

STEP 6 Sketch in the fences that you will later screw to the front and back edges of the box. On mine the curves are drawn around the base of a can of spray paint.

STEP 7 Most of the cuts on the fences could be made on the band saw, but some, however, had to be cut with a saber saw.

STEP 8 Invert the box on your table saw and screw the fences in place.

STEP 9 Place the box right-side up with the maple strips in the miter gauge slots and make a saw cut which goes entirely through the plywood base and partially through the two cherry fences. Notice that this cut will allow you to crosscut stock that is about ¾" thick. You could raise the blade even more in order to cut thicker stock, but doing so would weaken the cutoff box. Wider and thicker fences should be used for a cutoff box intended to crosscut thicker material.

STEP 10 Turn the handle with which you will push the box back and forth on your table saw.

STEP 11 Before attaching the top support piece, glue the handle tenon in place on the support piece, wedging the tenon on the bottom side.

27

STEP **12** Fasten the support piece in place with four 3½" no.12 wood screws.

STEP **13** In this photo, I'm using the cutoff box to crosscut the ends of a glued up cherry panel I used for a tabletop.

Here is the completed table, the top of which I'm shown cutting in step 13.

PHOTO CREDIT: GARRY FRAZIER

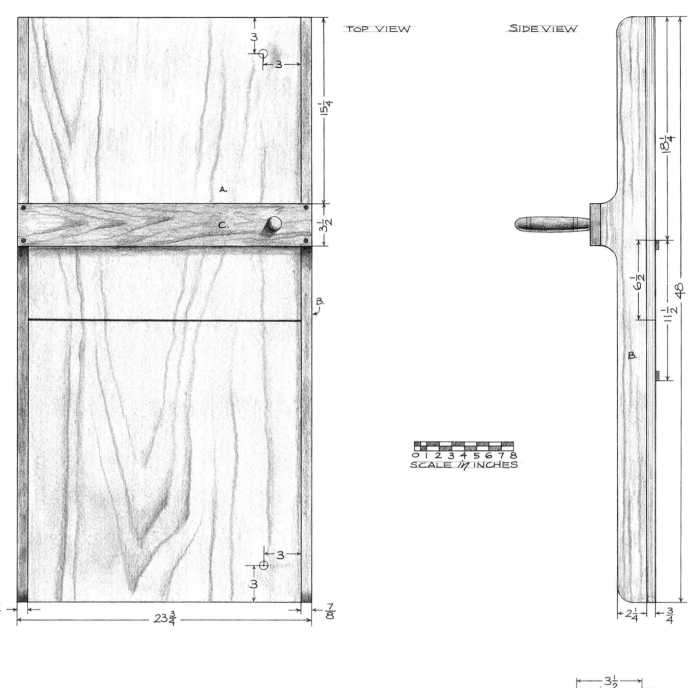

TOP VIEW

3
3
3

15¼

A.

C.

3½

B.

3
3

⅞
23¾
⅞

SIDE VIEW

18¼

6½

11½
48

B.

2¼
¾

SCALE *in* INCHES
0 1 2 3 4 5 6 7 8

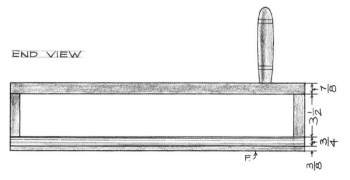

END VIEW

⅞
3½
¾
F.
⅜

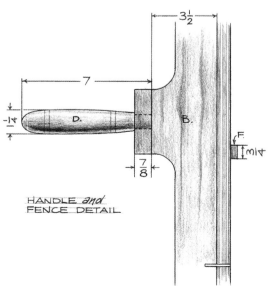

3½

7

¼

D.

B.

F.
3¼

⅞

HANDLE *and*
FENCE DETAIL

INCHES (MILLIMETERS)

REFERENCE	QUANTITY	PART	STOCK	THICKNESS	(mm)	WIDTH	(mm)	LENGTH	(mm)
A	1	deck		3/4	(19)	22 3/4	(578)	48	(1219)
B	2	fence		7/8	(22)	3 1/2	(89)	48	(1219)
C	1	top		7/8	(22)	3 1/2	(89)	23 3/4	(603)

HARDWARE & SUPPLIES

1 1/4" x 7" (32mm x 178mm) handle (including tenon)

2 1/8" x 3/4" x 3/4" (3mm x 19mm x 19mm) wedges

2 3/8" x 3/4" x 23 3/4" (10mm x 19mm x 603mm) strips

Raised-Panel Jig

You can create raised panels on a shaper with some really big cutters, but it is a little better, I think, to cut them on the table saw because, instead of ejecting the waste into the air in the form of chips and dust, a table-saw jig removes the waste in the form of thin strips of solid wood.

This table-saw jig will allow you to create almost any style of raised panel with a minimum of ejected waste.

When using the table saw to create finished surfaces, as I'm doing here, I use a hollow-ground planer blade because it leaves behind a smooth surface almost devoid of saw marks.

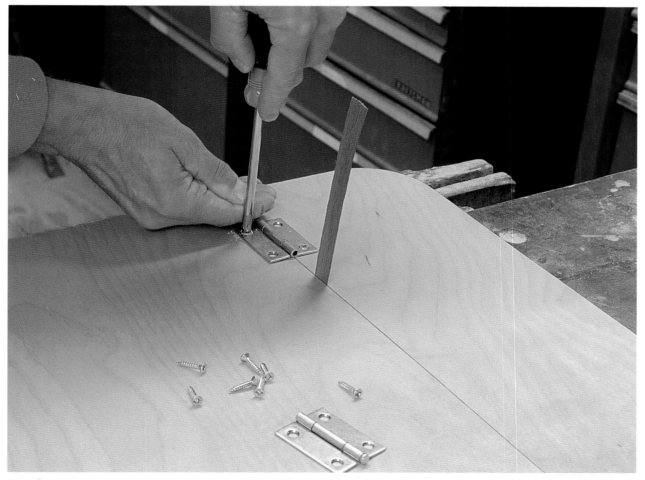

STEP 1 Start work by fastening together the horizontal leaf and the vertical leaf with a pair of steel hinges. (The strips of veneer allow me to maintain a consistent amount of clearance along the full length of the jig.)

STEP 2 With a compass, sketch in the support brackets for the vertical leaf. These will be screwed to small cleats which, in turn, will be screwed to the horizontal leaf. The adjustment bolt penetrates the bracket on the vertical leaf and rides in the curved notch in the bracket screwed to the horizontal leaf. Cut the terminus of the curved notch with a Forstner bit.

STEP 3 Cut the notch itself on the band saw.

STEP 4 Fabricate the bracket which you will later screw to the vertical leaf, as well as the cleat with which you'll fasten the bracket to the leaf.

STEP 5 Then, screw the cleat to the vertical leaf.

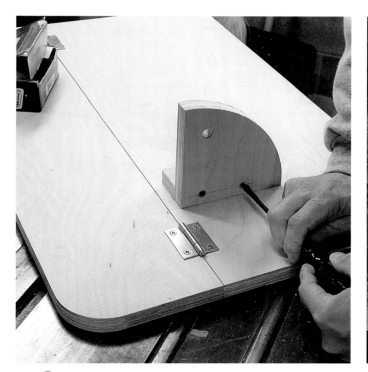

STEP **6** Screw the bracket to the cleat.

STEP **7** Using the bracket on the vertical leaf as a guide, determine where to place the cleat that will mount the bracket on the horizontal leaf.

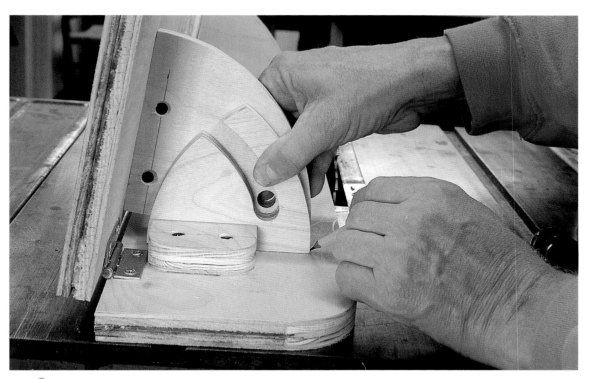

STEP **8** After screwing that cleat into place, determine where to fasten the bracket on the horizontal leaf. It should be placed so that the hole in the bracket mounted on the vertical leaf is centered in the notch cut in the bracket mounted on the horizontal leaf.

STEP 9 Then, turn your attention to the blade guard. A guard is necessary because more than a third of the table saw blade will be exposed when this jig is being used. The guard is built around two pieces of a length of 2 x 6. A thin Plexiglass strip is then screwed to the guard to protect your fingers from the blade while still allowing you to see what's going on.

In this photo, I'm cutting the Plexiglass shield on the band saw. I've left the blue protective plastic in place while I cut and shape this strip.

STEP 10 The Plexiglass strip can be slid from side to side to better cover the blade using mounting screws which pass through two elongated holes in the Plexiglass. Start the notches by first drilling a hole at either end of each notch.

STEP 11 Then, with a mortise chisel, connect the holes, in this manner creating the elongated holes.

STEP 12 Then, screw the Plexiglass to the guard.

STEP 13 Fasten the jig and the blade guard to the saw with clamps as shown.

STEP 14 It would be very difficult for your fingers to make contact with the saw blade.

STEP 15 Set up the jig by placing it in the approximate location on the saw table. Then measure from two points along the miter-gauge slot to the jig. It's important to measure from two points because the jig must be parallel to the miter gauge slot and therefore the blade. If it isn't, the heel of the blade may dig into the work leaving behind unsightly saw marks that will be difficult to clean up with hand tools.

Once the jig is the correct distance from and parallel to the miter gauge slots, clamp the jig into its position. Then slide the guard close enough to the work so that there is no gap into which fingers might fall. Clamp the guard in place. Slide the work into the blade, keeping your fingers high up on the work.

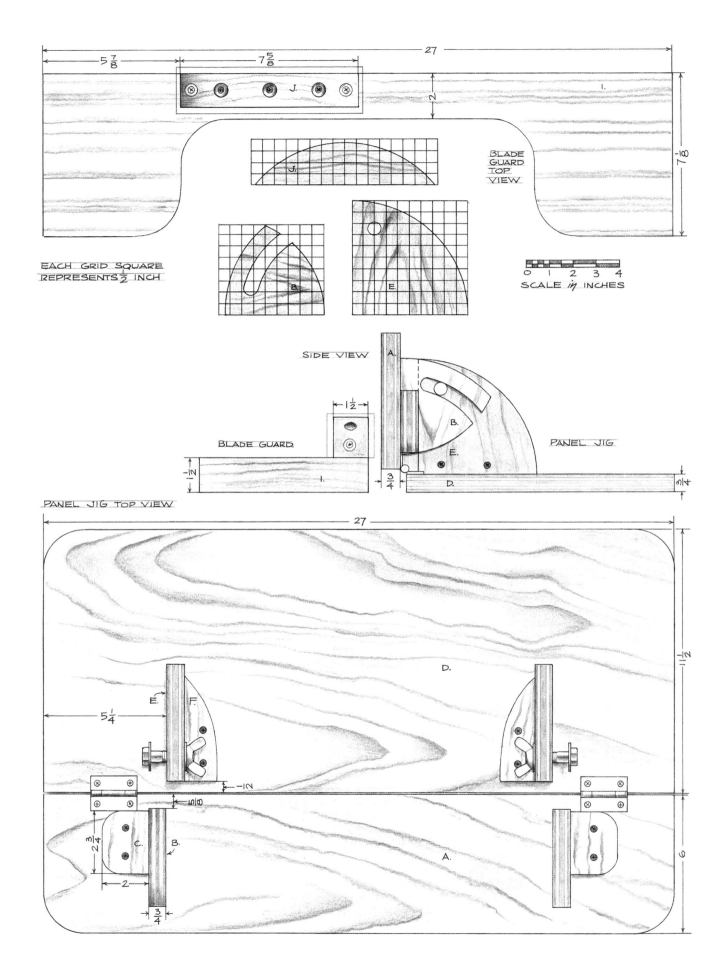

EACH GRID SQUARE
REPRESENTS ½ INCH

BLADE
GUARD
TOP
VIEW

J.

B.

E.

J.

0 1 2 3 4
SCALE *in* INCHES

SIDE VIEW

A.

B.

E.

BLADE GUARD

PANEL JIG

I.

D.

PANEL JIG TOP VIEW

27

11½

D.

E.

F.

5¼

A.

B.

C.

2

¾

6

INCHES (MILLIMETERS)

REFERENCE	QUANTITY	PART	STOCK	THICKNESS	(mm)	WIDTH	(mm)	LENGTH	(mm)
A	1	horizontal leaf		3/4	(19)	6	(152)	27	(686)
B	2	horizontal leaf brackets		3/4	(19)	4	(102)	4 1/4	(108)
C	2	horizontal leaf cleats		3/4	(19)	2	(51)	2 3/4	(70)
D	1	vertical leaf		3/4	(19)	11 1/2	(292)	27	(686)
E	2	vertical leaf brackets		3/4	(19)	5	(127)	5	(127)
F	2	vertical leaf cleats		3/4	(19)	1 7/16	(36)	4 1/2	(115)

HARDWARE & SUPPLIES

22" x 1 1/2" (51mm x 38mm) hinges

11 1/2" x 7 1/8" x 27" (38mm x 181mm x 686mm) blade guard base

11 1/2" x 1 7/8" x 7 11/16" (38mm x 47mm x 196mm) curved Plexiglass support

1 1/8" x 1 3/4" x 9" (3mm x 45mm x 229mm) Plexiglass

Jig for Cutting Tenons on Curved Legs

I build lots of Shaker tripod tables. When I began making them, I cut the tenons on the ends of the legs the old-fashioned way: by hand. Sometimes these tenons were in the form of sliding dovetails. Sometimes they were simple tenons. Eventually, I decided that the little bit of extra strength these dovetails provided was not worth the effort they required.

I also decided that the simple tenons I had been cutting laboriously by hand with a backsaw could be more efficiently cut on the table saw.

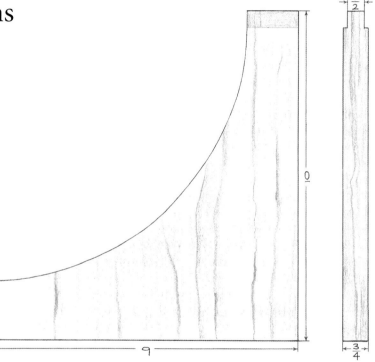

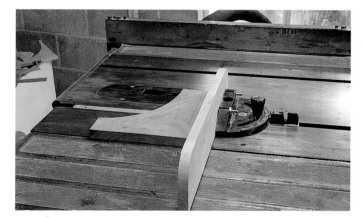

STEP 1 The jig is nothing more than the scrap left behind after cutting out the band sawn profile of a curved leg.

STEP 2 The leg is pressed up against the scrap which is itself pressed up against the wood miter gauge extension. The only difficulty of using this jig is this: To align the jig and the leg it holds with the stack of dado cutters, the saw operator has to lean forward far enough to sight the leading edge of the leg being tenoned as it approaches the blade.

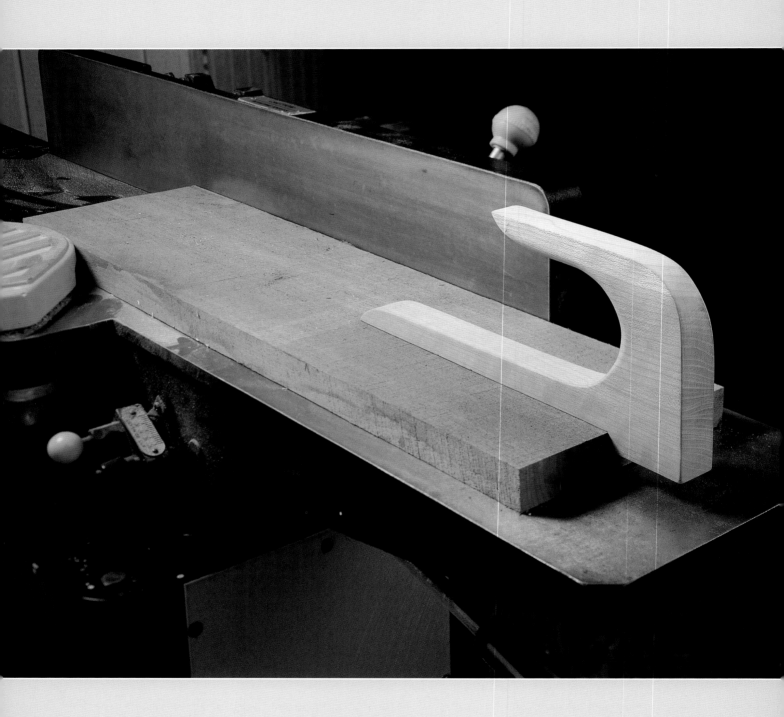

CHAPTER THREE

Stock-feeding Aides

Thirty years ago, I took a job as the yard supervisor for Seneca Lumber and Millwork in my hometown of Fostoria, Ohio. The title "supervisor" was an honorific I had been assigned to distract me from the fact that I was doing — usually by myself — the hard physical labor of loading customers' trucks while earning just a bit more than minimum wage.

Seneca Lumber's retail yard shared a group of connected buildings with the company's mill, which had a national reputation for bow windows and residential circular stairways, as well as high-end custom architectural work of almost any kind.

The mill employed a dozen men. Some were highly accomplished craftsmen. Others were only marginally skilled, incapable of much more than feeding stair tread and riser stock to a table saw or a planer.

I often had lunch with the men from the mill, and as I got to know them, I noticed that several had missing fingers or missing parts of fingers, injuries which were oddly most common among the least skilled of the mill's employees. I then learned that — in almost every case — these digits had been claimed by the table saws and planers manned by those least skilled employees.

Although Seneca Lumber and Millwork is now long gone, I've noticed in other mills I've visited in recent years a greater percentage of employees with a full complement of digits on each hand.

Why? The answer is obvious enough that even I can see it. Over the last 30 years, thanks in part to the work of governmental regulatory agencies like OSHA, woodworking shops have begun to pay more attention to safety. On the shop floor, this increased attention translates to — among other things — power stock feeders (which remove most of the danger for the men and women operating table saws, planers, and molders). And those machines not equipped with power feeders have push sticks and push blocks stored conveniently close by.

This, I think, is a good thing.

Push Block

A push block is a purely functional device, intended to make it possible for a machine operator to move material past a cutting tool without getting the operator's fingers too close to the business end of the cutting tool.

But the fact that it's a functional device doesn't mean that it can't also be attractive. This is something for which the Shakers were justifiably renowned. It was standard practice for Shaker furniture makers to add a measure of beauty to otherwise purely functional shop-made tools.

This little push block meets the usefulness criteria, and it is also an attractive little piece which, I think, has a sculpted feel.

STEP 1 Sketch the outline of the push block on a piece of wood. Because the handle is unsupported on the front edge, there is a possibility of the handle breaking along the grain in the column of wood that supports the upper part of the push block. For that reason, I made that column of wood a little wider than I would have otherwise.

STEP 2 Cut out the shape on the band saw.

STEP 3 I consciously made the inside curve on the column of wood that supported the upper handle a bit wider than the front wheel on my sander. This allowed me to use the sander to clean up saw marks on this curved surface.

STEP 4 Take the push block in your hand the way you will hold it in operation. Then make marks indicating the limits of hand-and-push-block contact. Relieve the corners between these marks to make the push block fit your hand more comfortably.

STEP 5 Use a carving chisel to rough in these rounds.

STEP 6 Finish the process with a rasp followed by sandpaper.

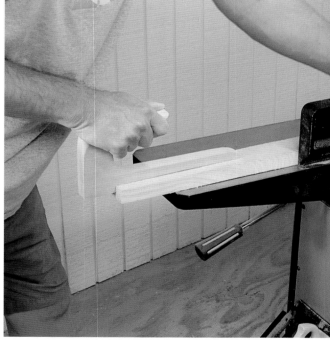

STEP 7 Here's the push block in action. In my left hand, I'm holding a foam-bottomed push block to bear down on the material as it passes over the cutting head of my jointer. The recently finished push block in my right hand has a step on its bottom side which allows me to push the stock forward over the cutting head.

Push Sticks

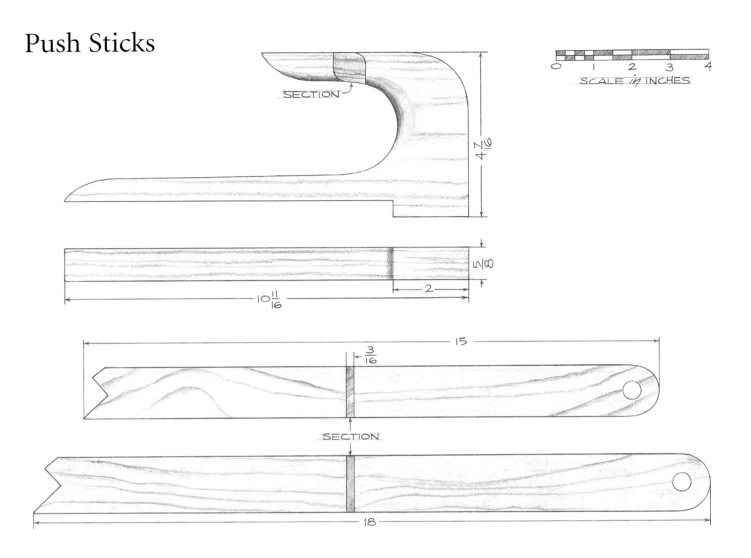

SECTION

$4\frac{7}{16}$

$\frac{5}{8}$

$10\frac{11}{16}$

2

SCALE *in* INCHES

0   1   2   3   4

15

$\frac{3}{16}$

SECTION

18

I've used lots of different hardwoods for push sticks. Cherry, which is fairly brittle, is not a good choice. Hard maple is much better, and ash, I think, is best because of its enormous strength even when cut to fairly fine dimensions. My push sticks always have a little bird's mouth in one end to grip the edge of a piece of material.

This is the way I rip material using a pair of push sticks. Notice that I'm not standing directly behind the work. In that manner, I avoid being impaled by a piece of material thrown back at me by an angry table saw. Notice, too, that the push sticks allow me to keep my hands well away from the table saw blade.

As I Say, Not As I Do

Four years ago, I was lucky enough to have two of my chairs shown as part of a furniture-making exhibition at the Decorative Arts Center of Ohio. The show's opening included an evening wine-and-cheese event for several hundred patrons of the center. That morning, I was using a set of dado cutters to plough grooves in some short lengths of cherry for a Shaker-inspired sewing desk. Because my push blocks weren't where I usually keep them, and I was too lazy to search them out, I was feeding the stock with my hands. I was in a hurry. I'd had a frustrating morning during which I had managed to make every conceivable workshop mistake.

The first dozen pieces in which I ploughed grooves sailed smoothly across my dado cutters, but then, for no reason I could see at the time and for no reason I could see later in retrospect, one of those short lengths of cherry reared up on its end. And my thumb, with which I'd been pressing the stock flat against my table saw, slid down the short length of cherry toward the dado cutters.

I believe there was a microsecond during which I knew what was happening and what was going to happen. I can remember my brain sending out a message to the muscles in my arm to retract, to pull my thumb back. But my body was too slow and my thumb lurched down along the length of cherry that was now standing on end, being chewed up by the coarse carbide teeth of my dado cutters, rattling against the table saw's rip fence. And then my thumb, too, was being chewed by those coarse carbide teeth.

Well, the message finally got through, and I yanked my thumb up, too late of course, out of harm's way. With my other hand, I reached down automatically to the cutoff switch bringing the saw to a stop. Then, I pushed my way through the shop door, jumped two steps down to ground level and, still without looking at my thumb because I knew what I was going to see there, I ran a half dozen strides out into the driveway and stopped. There was no one home but me. I'd have to drive myself to the hospital. I thought how awkward that would be, one hand mangled, the other applying pressure. Then I clutched my mangled thumb in my other hand applying pressure to the wound, and finally with my damaged thumb half hidden by the hand that was applying pressure, I looked down. Blood trailed along my forearm and trickled thickly onto the driveway, puddling there, not, I decided, arterial blood. It wasn't flowing that fast. But there was still a lot of blood. At first there was no pain — just anger, embarrassment, frustration. Then, as if somebody had thrown a switch, a blinding hammer of pain began to strike at the damaged thumb.

Cursing my stupidity, I moved toward the house, still applying pressure to the wound. Up the stairs, across the porch, I elbowed my way into the living room. I tried to cup the good hand under my thumb to catch the blood because I knew it would ruin the carpet. Then I was in the bathroom. Under running water, I kept pressure on the thumb for a few minutes, then a few minutes more. I realized then that the bleeding had slowed. The pain was worse, but the bleeding had slowed.

For the first time, I took away the other hand and really looked at what the dado cutters had done. It was ugly. A fleshy groove maybe 3/8" deep had been ploughed in the end of my thumb, right through the nail. I turned the thumb over but I was pretty sure the cutter had missed the bone.

That evening, in my best clothes, in the company of my wife, who had given me the scolding I deserved, with my thumb in a gauze wrapping the size of a grapefruit, I attended the opening of the Ohio-Furniture-by-Contemporary-Masters exhibition. Several of the craftsmen whose work was on display there asked about my bandage, and when I explained, they made courteous expressions of sympathy, but I know what they were thinking: "You were feeding stock over your dado cutters barehanded? What are you doing in this exhibition?"

I was very lucky. I made a bad decision while operating what I believe to be the most dangerous tool in my shop. Nevertheless, except for some permanent numbness in part of my thumb, I suffered no lasting damage. I think that's why the stock-feeding aides in this chapter are so important. We woodworkers shouldn't rely on luck to keep us safe because ours is an inherently dangerous avocation.

CHAPTER FOUR

Lathe Aides

I'm not a great turner. I'm probably not even a good turner, but I am an efficient turner, and much of my efficiency at the lathe is a result of two different lathe aides I have constructed. One is a simple marking gauge that allows me to accurately divide the outside surface of turned cylinders, which is essential for the many lathe-based pieces I build each year.

But it is the length-of-part tool rest that is responsible for most of my efficiency at the lathe, making it possible for me to turn very quickly the many simple Shaker forms I produce. In the past decade, I've probably made a dozen of these rests, some not much longer than the factory rest that came with my lathe and some, which I use for turned chair back posts, measuring over 44" in length.

Length-of-Part Tool Rests

Many years ago, when I began making Shaker reproduction chairs, I had what I thought was a big idea about how I might make better use of my time at the lathe. Unlike most of my big ideas (which turn out in actual fact to be small ideas) this one turned out to be as big in fact as it had been in my imagination.

Instead of repeatedly loosening, positioning, and retightening the factory tool rest on my lathe as I worked my way along the length of turned chair parts (some back posts are 44" long and the factory rest is only 12" long), I decided to make length-of-part tool-

rests which need to be positioned only once for each part. In fact, if I'm turning a bunch of parts of the same length say, for example, front rungs for a set of dining chairs I may turn 15 or 20 parts without moving my tool rest even once.

My first homemade tool rests weren't much, just a bar of hickory or ash constructed so that the top of the bar was the same height as the axis of rotation on my lathe. They weren't much, but they did what they were designed to do. I could work my way along the full length of a chair post without ever stopping the work to

reposition the tool rest.

In the intervening years, I've refined these rests, and the rests I now use are vastly superior to those first efforts. Instead of a flat top surface ¾" wide, my current rests have a top surface that is cut at an angle, mimicking the shape of the factory rest that came with my tool. Also, my current rests have more support for the upright arms that carry the actual rest. This extra support makes the rests more rigid. I eventually became comfortable with the springiness of those first rests, but the rigidity of my newer versions is comforting.

STEP 1 I believe that ash and hickory are the very best choices for a jig in which strength is critical. This particular tool rest was made from this length of ash. Notice that this piece of wood contains the pith, the heart of the tree. Like all wood from the pith, this piece is deeply checked.

STEP 2 I ripped 2" strips from the ash. Those sections marked by splits I tossed into my burn box, but I was able to use material from above and below the checks.

STEP 3 After jointing and planing the 2" strips, use your jointer to cut a bevel on the rest's horizontal bar. This shape is critical because it enables the lathe tool to be supported close to the spinning work.

For reasons of safety, it is imperative that a tool rest provide support for the tool as close as possible to the part being turned. If the distance between the support and the work is too great, the tool can catch on the work and be driven down into the gap between the support and the work with potentially disastrous results. Although I never had an accident of this type with my earlier versions of this rest, it is comforting to know that my current versions take that risk into account.

STEP 4 Transfer the angle from the rest's horizontal bar to the top of the support posts using a bevel gauge.

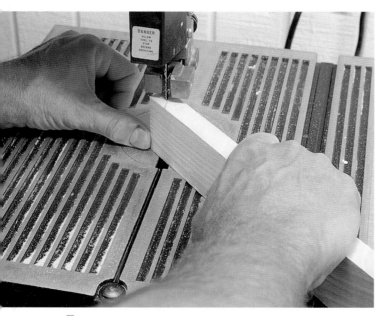

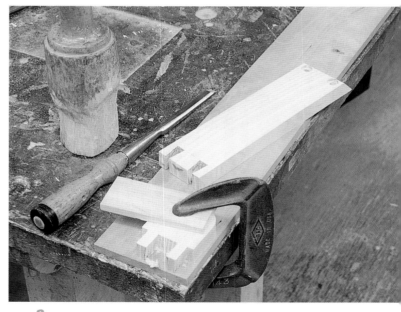

STEP 5 Cut that angle on the band saw.

STEP 6 Then, cut a quick set of through dovetails to connect the bottom of the support post with the jig's foot.

STEP 7 After gluing and assembling the dovetails, sand the base of the foot square.

STEP 8 Finally, add these ¼" thick stiffener panels to each of the support posts.

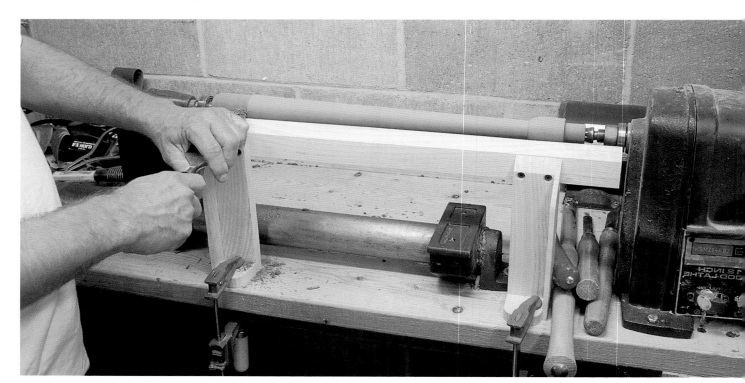

STEP 9 Once you have worked with length-of-part tool rests, you will never go back to the old way of turning.

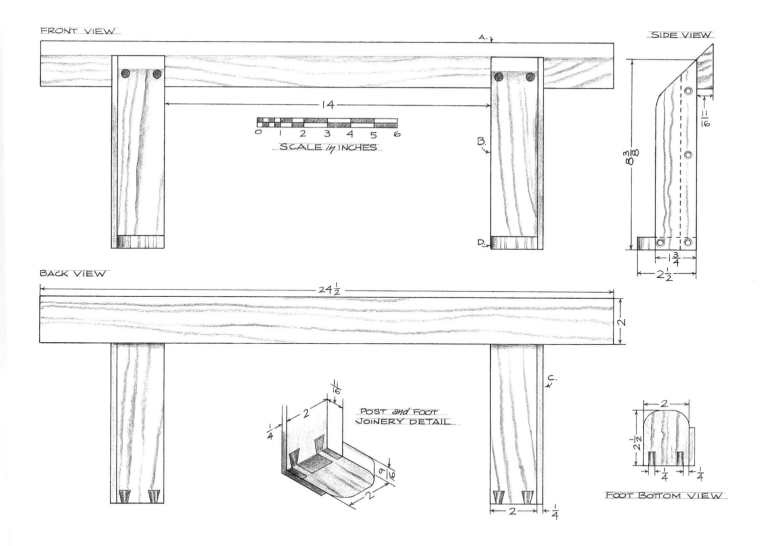

FRONT VIEW

A.

SIDE VIEW

14

SCALE in INCHES
0 1 2 3 4 5 6

B.

D.

$8\frac{3}{8}$

$\frac{11}{16}$

$1\frac{3}{4}$

$2\frac{1}{2}$

BACK VIEW

$24\frac{1}{2}$

2

C.

$\frac{11}{16}$

2

$\frac{1}{4}$

POST and FOOT
JOINERY DETAIL

$\frac{9}{16}$

2

2

$\frac{1}{4}$

2

$2\frac{1}{2}$

$\frac{1}{4}$ $\frac{1}{4}$

FOOT BOTTOM VIEW

2

$\frac{1}{4}$

INCHES (MILLIMETERS)

REFERENCE	QUANTITY	PART	STOCK	THICKNESS	(mm)	WIDTH	(mm)	LENGTH	(mm)
A	1	horizontal bar		$\frac{11}{16}$	(18)	2	(51)	$24\frac{1}{2}$	(623)
B	2	support posts		$\frac{11}{16}$	(18)	2	(51)	$8\frac{3}{8}$	(213)
C	2	post stiffeners		$\frac{1}{4}$	(6)	$1\frac{3}{4}$	(45)	$8\frac{3}{8}$	(213)
D	2	foot		$\frac{9}{16}$	(14)	2	(51)	$2\frac{1}{2}$	(64)

49

Marking Gauge

Much of the work done in my shop is lathe-based. For every piece of casework I create, I probably make a dozen chairs or tripod tables — all constructions which begin life on the lathe.

That means I must have ways to quickly and accurately mark parts which have been turned on the lathe.

To accomplish this, I built a lathe marking gauge which allows me to draw lines on the outside diameter of a turned part that are parallel to the part's axis of rotation.

The gauge is nothing more than a vertical post which holds a pencil at the same height above my lathe bed as the lathe's axis of rotation.

My gauge has a flat-bottomed foot because my lathe bed is a deck of 2 × 6's. Your version of the gauge might have a different base, one accommodating whatever style lathe bed you have. All you need is a construction that will allow you to hold a pencil at a height above your lathe bed that is equal to your lathe's axis of rotation.

STEP 1 Start with the base. Once you've decided what kind of foot will work best on your lathe, sketch in the shape on a piece of hardwood.

STEP 2 Spray cans, paint bottles, coffee cans — all of these make good layout aides.

STEP 3 After you've ripped out, planed, and cut to length the gauge's post, drill the hole for the pencil. This hole should be small enough so that the pencil is held securely but not so small that it can't be inserted without force. Experiment with holes in scrap before you drill in the post.

STEP 4 Then, rotate the post 90° and drill the hole for the set screw that will hold the pencil in place. Again, the best way to determine the right hole size is to experiment on scrap. Find a hole size that is small enough to allow the threads on the screw to engage the walls of the hole but not so small that the screw is twisted off when you turn it into the hole.

STEP 5 Fasten the post to the base with a single screw. (The thick notch will hold it square.) I've recessed the screw head for aesthetic reasons.

STEP 6 Here's the completed gauge, ready for use.

STEP 7 The gauge holds the pencil point at the same height as my lathe's axis of rotation. Once I've locked the lathe's indexing head, I can use this gauge to make marks on the outside diameter of a turned object that are parallel to the object's axis of rotation.

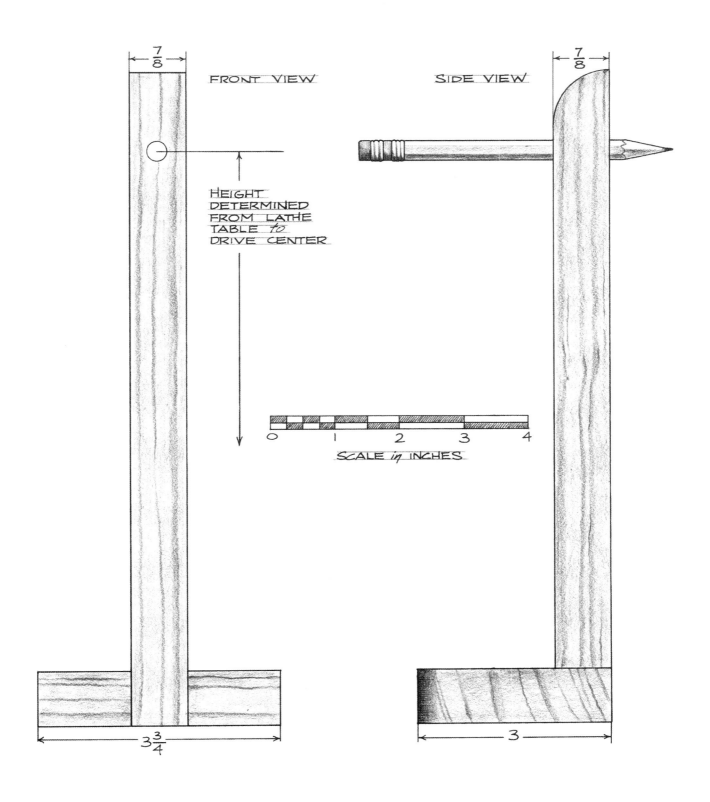

FRONT VIEW

7/8

HEIGHT
DETERMINED
FROM LATHE
TABLE to
DRIVE CENTER

3 3/4

SIDE VIEW

7/8

0 1 2 3 4

SCALE in INCHES

3

INCHES (MILLIMETERS)

REFERENCE	QUANTITY	PART	STOCK	THICKNESS	(mm)	WIDTH	(mm)	LENGTH	(mm)
A	1	base		7/8	(22)	3	(76)	3 3/4	(95)
B	1	post		7/8	(22)	7/8	(22)	10 1/2	(267)

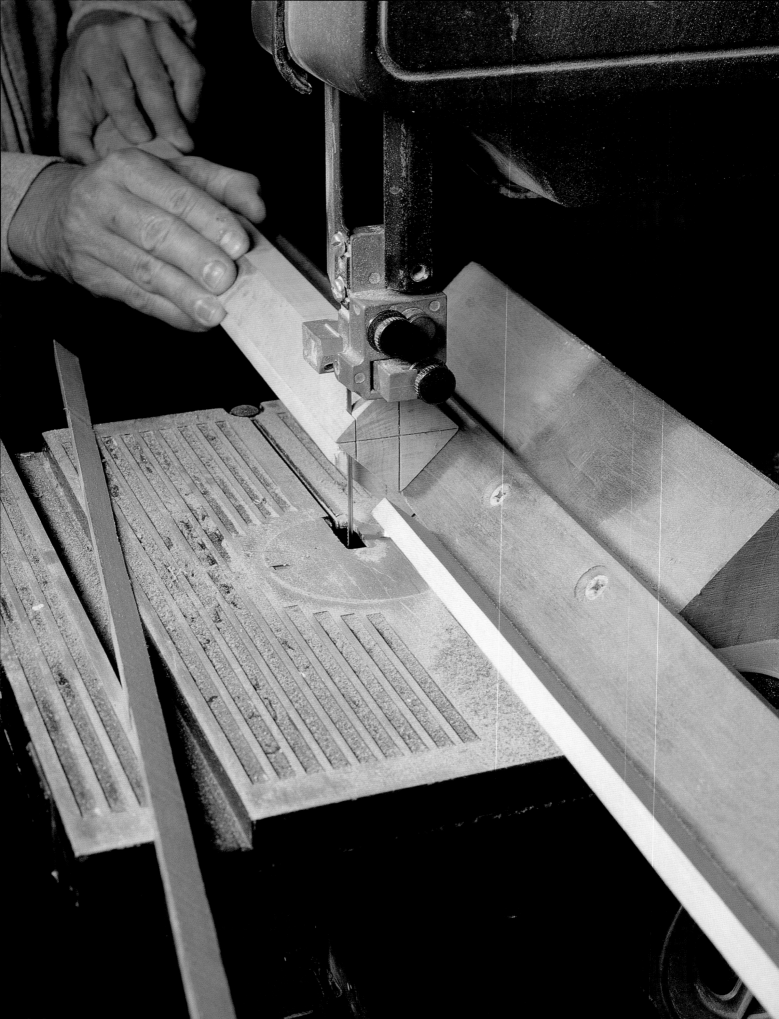

CHAPTER FIVE

Band Saw Aides

I spend a lot of time at the band saw. Some of that time is spent doing the work for which the band saw is specifically designed, that is sawing curves and resawing stock to thinner dimensions. But most of my time at the band saw is spent transforming stock that is square in cross section to stock that is octagonal in cross section. This refined shape simplifies the turning process because the octagonal stock more closely resembles the round shapes ultimately created on the lathe.

Cradle #1

This cradle is designed to pass under the blade along with the work which it supports. It's what I reach for when I want to quickly prepare a short length of turning stock.

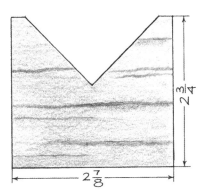

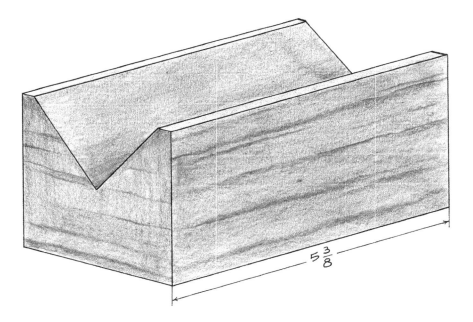

STEP 1 Sketch an X on the end grain of your V-block stock. If the stock is square, the material you'll excise will be a right triangle in cross section, leaving an opening perfectly suited for stabilizing a square turning blank as it's passed under the blade.

STEP 2 With the block standing on end, cut out one quarter of the X.

STEP 3 I laid the cut corners on my belt sander to flatten the sharp, and therefore fragile, corners.

STEP 4 Draw lines on your square turning stock as shown. Then use the cradle to support the stock while you pass it under the blade. Make sure you center (incise the X's on the end grain of) your turning block before you cut away the corners. Otherwise, you won't be able to accurately position the work against the blade to cut from corner to corner.

Cradle #2

The blanks from which I turn chair posts are much too long to be passed under the blade held in a moveable cradle. For making octagons of long stock, I use this jig which can support lengthy material on its generous infeed and outfeed decks so that the stock is slid along the cradle past the blade.

STEP 1 Start with the base. Screw a length of ⁵⁄₁₆" thick stock to one side of a length of hardwood that is a right triangle in cross section. (I actually used two short lengths of cherry here because I didn't have one piece that was long enough.) That ⁵⁄₁₆" material will form the base of this jig. This base will ultimately be clamped to the table of your band saw.

STEP 2 Screw a length of ¾" material to another face of the triangular-in-cross-section rips. The ¾" thickness is necessary because this portion of the cradle deck will support the other deck along with the stock being converted to an octagon.

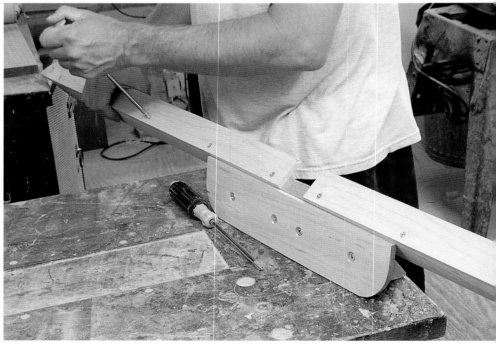

STEP 3 Screw a pair of ⁵⁄₁₆" thick strips to the bottom edge of the ¾" stock. These pieces will form the cradle's other deck. The stock being converted to an octagon will slide past the blade between the two decks. Notice the gap between these strips. The band saw blade will fit into this gap.

STEP 4 In order to set up this jig, you need to find the angle of drift for your band saw blade. Do this with a piece of thin material on which you have drawn a straight line. Feed the material past the blade, keeping the blade in the center of that straight line.

What you'll notice is that, in order to keep the blade on that straight line, you've had to feed the stock at an angle when compared to one side of the band saw table. That angle is the angle of drift for your band saw blade. Unfortunately, you can't use the same angle of drift for the next blade you install in your tool because every blade has its own cutting signature, which creates a separate angle of drift.

To set up this jig, lay a second piece of material on your band saw table that is parallel with the edge of the table. Push one end of this second piece against the same end of the piece which you've fed past the blade. Then, take a measurement at the front of the table between the two pieces of thin material. The jig should be set so that its base is out of parallel with the edge of the band saw table an amount equal to that measurement.

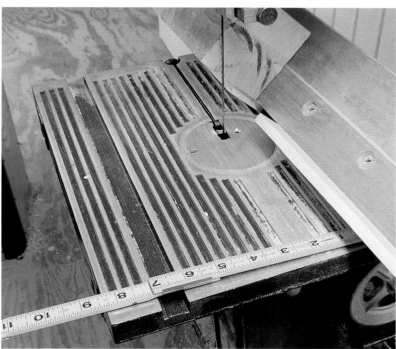

STEP 5 Set the jig in place so that, when the blade is set to remove the desired amount from the turning blank, the base of the jig is out of parallel to the front edge of the band saw table an amount that is equal to the amount out of parallel of the thin stock you cut in the previous photo. This will align the jig with the blade's angle of drift.

STEP 6 This photo shows one of the clamps that hold the jig to the band saw table in the required position. The clamps can be loosened to allow minute adjustments in jig placement.

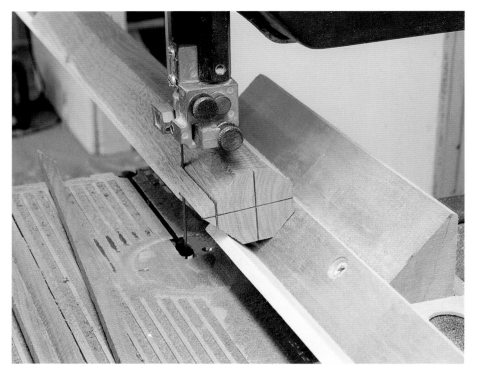

Tips for Sawing Octagons

Be patient if you're using the second jig. Because of the angle-of-drift issue, this jig can be a little fussy to set up.

• Even if you've accurately determined your blade's angle of drift, it may be necessary to make minute adjustments of the jig's placement once you've begun cutting.

• Always work with a sharp blade. The most common bandsaw mistake I see is the use of a dull blade. You may need a new blade for every four or five hours you spend at the bandsaw, particularly if you're cutting tough woods like ash or hickory or oak. A dull bandsaw blade can't be made to behave, no matter how skillful the operator.

• Sawing these octagons requires a blade at least $1/4$" in width. Half-inch blades produce even better cutting, although I rarely take the time to install a $1/2$" blade since it requires me to reset the band saw's guide blocks.

• Feed the stock past the blade at a slow, steady pace. Feeding it too quickly will result in a wandering blade, even if the jig is set up properly and the blade is in good working order.

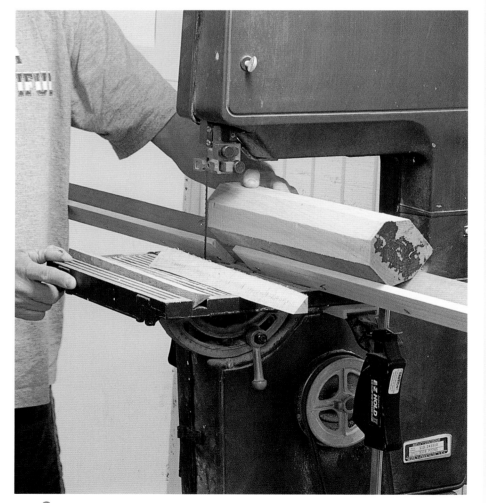

STEP **8** Here the jig is being used to create an octagon from a short length of cherry turning stock.

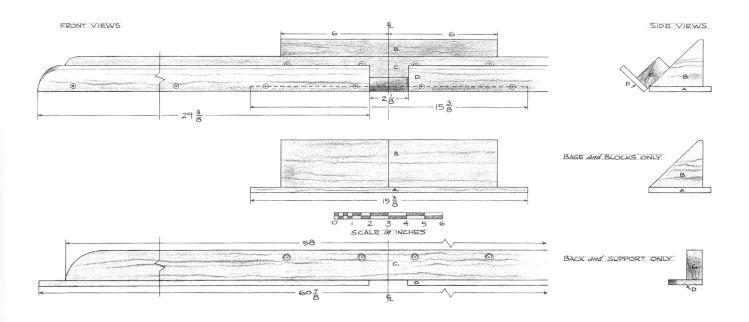

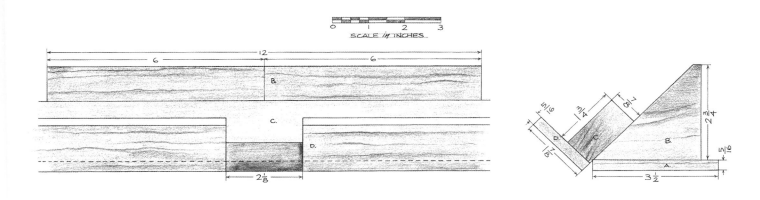

INCHES (MILLIMETERS)

REFERENCE	QUANTITY	PART	STOCK	THICKNESS	(mm)	WIDTH	(mm)	LENGTH	(mm)
A	1	base		$5/16$	(8)	$3^1/2$	(89)	$15^3/8$	(391)
B	2	blocks		$2^3/4$	(70)	3	(76)	6	(152)
C	1	back		$7/8$	(22)	$1^3/4$	(45)	58	(1473)
D	2	supports		$5/16$	(8)	$1^7/8$	(47)	$29^3/8$	(747)

CHAPTER SIX

Drill Press Aides

The key to successful post-and-rung chairmaking is drilling accurate rung mortises in the chair posts. These can be drilled freehand by clamping the chair parts in a vise, then engaging the bit in the post while a pair of spotters calls out the proper angles. It takes a pair of spotters because the rungs enter the posts at a compound angle. One spotter must check the angle from the side, while another spotter checks the angle from above.

But it's much easier to place the chair parts on a set of drill press jigs and to let the jigs to do all the fussy work of holding the parts in the proper alignment in regard to the drill bit.

Although the jigs in this chapter were designed to facilitate the accurate drilling of rung mortises on post-and-rung chairs, what I've found (over the ten years I've had them in my shop) is that they have other applications as well, some of which have little to do with chairmaking.

These jigs, like all the jigs and fixtures I have in my shop, have become important elements in my shop's problem-solving tool kit, and once you build them, I think they'll function in the same way in your shop.

INCHES (MILLIMETERS)

REFERENCE	QUANTITY	PART	STOCK	THICKNESS	(mm)	WIDTH	(mm)	LENGTH	(mm)
A	1	deck		3/4	(19)	23	(584)	20	(508)
B	1	fence		1 1/8	(29)	2	(51)	20	(508)

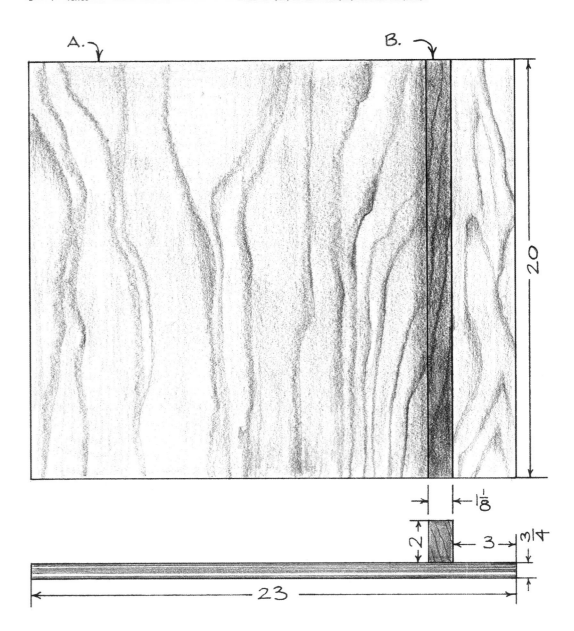

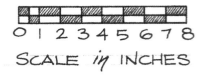

0 1 2 3 4 5 6 7 8

SCALE in INCHES

STEP 1 The simplest rung-mortise jig in my shop is nothing but a fence clamped to the wooden table of my drill press.

STEP 2 By placing that fence a distance from the lead point of my drill bit that is equal to half the diameter of a chair post, I'm able to bore front and back rung mortises in that chair post. In this photo, the fence is positioned for drilling mortises in post stock that is 1$\frac{3}{8}$" in diameter.

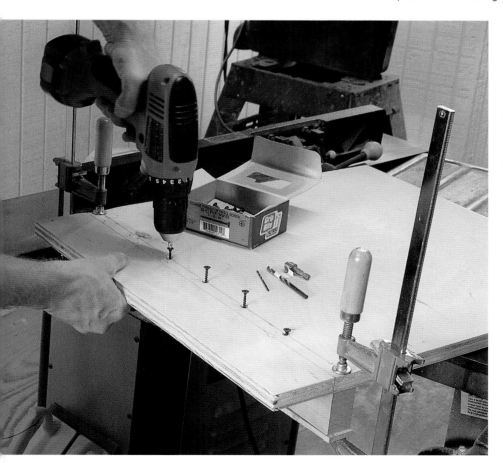

STEP 3 The side rung mortises for the Shaker stools I build require a slightly more complicated jig. These stools have side rungs which enter the posts 90° from the front and back rungs, so this jig consists of a simple fence screwed to a flat table I clamp to my drill-press table which is, itself, 90° from the axis of the drill bit.

The fence should be positioned so that there is sufficient width on the back table to allow me to clamp it to the drill press table and sufficient depth on the front table to accommodate the full width of the stool I'll be mortising on the jig. Once these parameters are established, screw the table to the bottom of the fence.

STEP 4 This table can also be used to drill the front rung mortises on any stools on which the side and front rungs are 90° apart. Once the jig is clamped to the drill press table, so that the fence is a distance from the lead point of my Forstner bit that is half the diameter of the post I'm mortising (see step 2 for fence placement) you can slide the ladder along the fence, stopping to bore mortises at the appropriate locations.

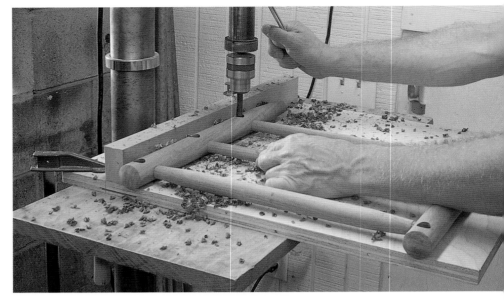

Front Rung Mortise Jig (FRMJ)

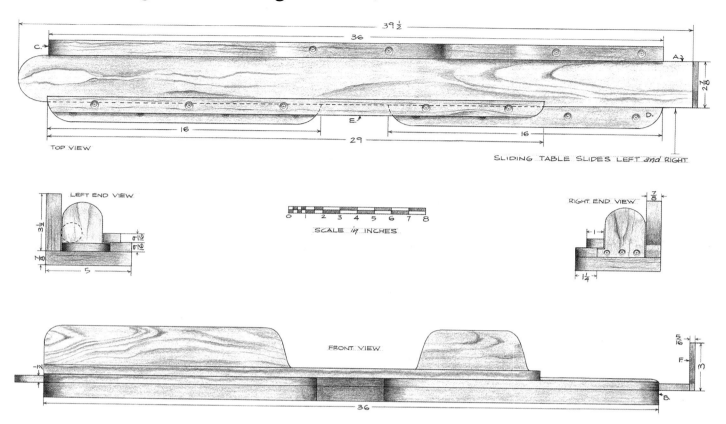

INCHES (MILLIMETERS)

REFERENCE	QUANTITY	PART	STOCK	THICKNESS	(mm)	WIDTH	(mm)	LENGTH	(mm)
A	1	sliding carriage		$^1/_2$	(13)	$2^7/_8$	(73)	$39^1/_2$	(1004)
B	1	jig bed		$^7/_8$	(22)	5	(127)	36	(914)
C	1	fence		$^7/_8$	(22)	$3^1/_2$	(89)	$39^1/_2$	(1004)
D	2	lower cleats		$^9/_{16}$	(14)	$1^1/_4$	(32)	16	(406)
E	1	top cleat		$^9/_{16}$	(14)	1	(25)	29	(737)
F	1	tail piece		$^5/_{16}$	(8)	$2^7/_8$	(73)	3	(76)

It's possible to drill the front rung mortises by pressing the post against a fence (see step 1), and for many years, I used a jig much like that for performing this operation. But eventually I realized that the tiniest of discrepancies in post rotation, as I slid the post under the bit from one rung location to the next, could result in fairly sizable errors in rung angle. To remedy this, I built a front-rung-mortise jig that prevents the post from rotating as it's passed underneath the drill bit. This guarantees that the centerlines of all the rungs on one side of a chair ladder will lie in the same plane.

STEP **1** Begin by flattening a length of cherry to use as the sliding carriage on which chair posts will travel from side to side underneath the drill bit.

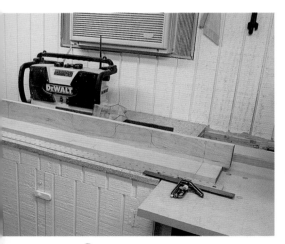

STEP **2** Then, set up the bed and fence of the jig, sketching in pencil the necessary band saw cuts.

STEP **3** After cutting out the parts and cleaning up sawmarks, screw (and glue) the fence to the back side of the jig bed.

STEP 4 Then, prepare the cleats that will hold the carriage in position against the back fence.

STEP 5 These cleats should be the barest fraction of an inch thicker than the sliding carriage. They should also be placed so that the carriage will slide freely between the cleats and the back fence.

STEP 6 When the cleats have been screwed in place, clean up any irregularities in fit between the front of the cleats and the front of the jig bed, using a couple of passes of a bench plane. Next, cut out and screw in place the top cleat which keeps the carriage locked in its track. Also screw the tail piece to the right end of the carriage.

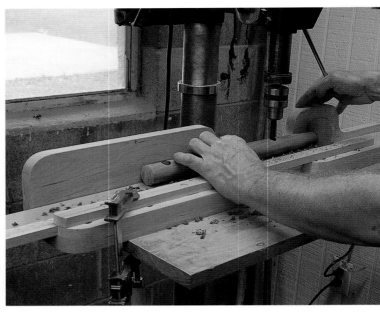

STEP 7 Once the jig has been clamped to the table (in a position that places the fence a distance from the lead point of my Forstner bit that is one half the diameter of the post to be mortised) load the post onto the sliding carriage. The post is prevented from rotating under the drill bit through the use of a pair of drywall screws which pass through the tail piece on the sliding carriage into the end grain of the post, as I'm doing in this photo.

STEP 8 Then, with the drill press quill set to bore a mortise $^{15}/_{16}$" deep, slide the carriage under the bit, stopping at each rung location.

STEP 9 This photo shows the difference in rung mortise accuracy between those drilled against a simple fence and those drilled using the front-rung-mortise jig. The mortises in the back post were drilled on the FRMJ. As a result the axes of all three rungs lie in the same plane. On the other hand, the mortises in the front post were drilled by sliding the post along a simple fence. As a result, the axis of each rung lies in a slightly different plane.

Although the error in mortise placement using a simple fence isn't sizable enough to create serious assembly problems, I prefer to depend on the accuracy of the FRMJ when performing this operation.

Side Rung Mortise Jig #2 (SRMJ)

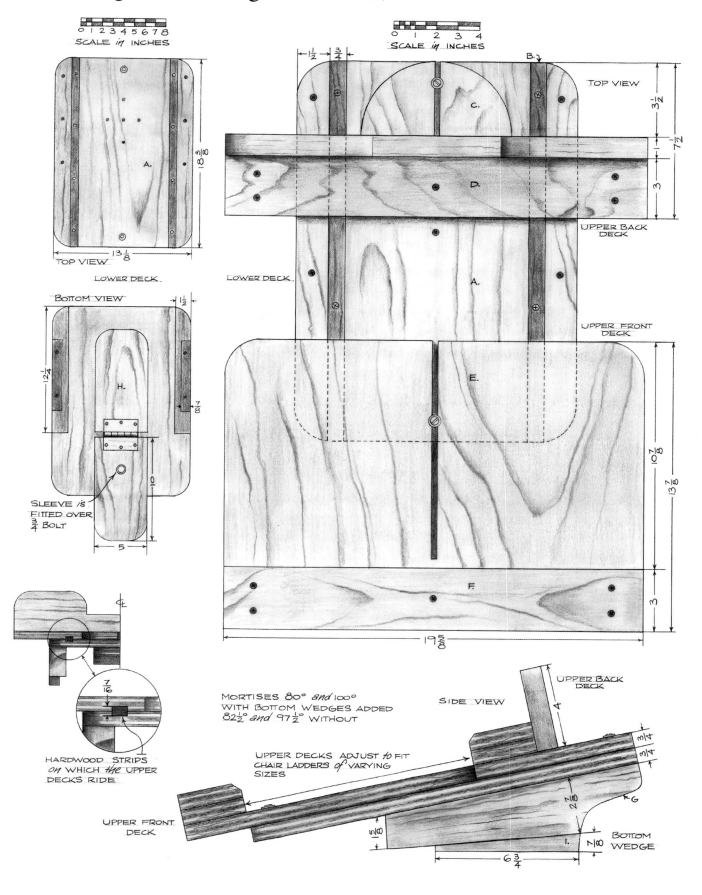

SCALE in INCHES
0 1 2 3 4 5 6 7 8

SCALE in INCHES
0 1 2 3 4

TOP VIEW

$18\frac{3}{8}$

A.

$13\frac{1}{8}$

TOP VIEW

LOWER DECK

BOTTOM VIEW

$12\frac{1}{4}$

H.

$1\frac{1}{2}$

$\frac{7}{8}$

SLEEVE is FITTED OVER $\frac{3}{4}$ BOLT

10

5

$\frac{7}{16}$

HARDWOOD STRIPS on WHICH the UPPER DECKS RIDE

$\frac{1}{2}$ $\frac{3}{4}$

B.

C.

$3\frac{1}{2}$

$7\frac{1}{2}$

1

D.

3

LOWER DECK

A.

UPPER BACK DECK

UPPER FRONT DECK

E.

$10\frac{7}{8}$

$13\frac{7}{8}$

F.

3

$19\frac{5}{8}$

MORTISES 80° and 100°
WITH BOTTOM WEDGES ADDED
$82\frac{1}{2}$° and $97\frac{1}{2}$° WITHOUT

UPPER DECKS ADJUST to FIT
CHAIR LADDERS of VARYING
SIZES

SIDE VIEW

UPPER BACK DECK

4

$\frac{3}{4}$
$\frac{3}{4}$

$2\frac{7}{8}$

G.

UPPER FRONT DECK

$\frac{5}{8}$

I.

$\frac{7}{8}$

BOTTOM WEDGE

$6\frac{3}{4}$

INCHES (MILLIMETERS)

REFERENCE	QUANTITY	PART	STOCK	THICKNESS	(mm)	WIDTH	(mm)	LENGTH	(mm)
A	1	lower deck		3/4	(19)	13 1/8	(333)	18 3/8	(467)
B	2	hardwood strips		7/16	(11)	3/4	(19)	18 3/8	(467)
C	1	upper back deck		3/4	(19)	7 1/2	(191)	19 5/8	(499)
D	2	fence deck ply sandwich		3/4	(19)	3	(76)	19 5/8	(499)
E	1	upper front deck		3/4	(19)	13	(330)	19 5/8	(499)
F	2	upper front deck sandwich		3/4	(19)	3	(76)	19 5/8	(499)
G	2	angled deck supports		7/8	(22)	2 7/8	(73)	12 3/4	(324)
H	2	wood hinge		3/4	(19)	5	(127)	10	(254)
I	2	angled support shims		7/8	(22)	7/8	(22)	6 3/4	(171)

HARDWARE & SUPPLIES

210" x 24" (254mm x 610mm) wood nuts

2 3/16" x 10" x 24" (5mm x 254mm x 610mm) machine screws

1 3/4" x 2 1/2" (19mm x 64mm) bolt with nut

All the Shaker chairs I build in my shop, and there are many different kinds, rely on one of two sets of side-rung angles.

The New Lebanon production chairs are assembled with side rungs, the axes of which are 97 1/2° from the axes of the back rungs and 82 1/2° from the axes of the front rungs.

Earlier, non-production chairs, have a slightly different set of side-rung angles. These chairs are assembled with side rungs, the axes of which are 100° from the axes of the back rungs and 80° from the axes of the front rungs. The difference is statistically slight but very noticeable when you sight a chair seat from above.

Because all the chairs I build rely on one of these two sets of angles, I didn't need a side-rung-mortise jig (SRMJ) that was infinitely adjustable. All I needed was a jig with two settings. I achieved this by constructing the jig so that, in its basic form, it gives me the angles required by the New Lebanon production chairs. The steeper angles required by the earlier chairs I achieve by screwing a pair of shims under the feet of my SRMJ.

STEP 1 Begin the construction by plowing the grooves into which you'll screw the hardwood guide strips that align the upper and lower decks.

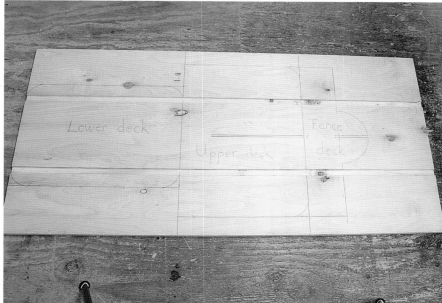

STEP 2 It's imperative that the grooves on the top of the plywood lower deck and on the bottoms of the jig's sliding decks match up perfectly. The best way to achieve that match is to cut them all at once as I've done here. In this photo, you can see that the three decks have been sketched in around the grooves.

STEP 3 Then, thickness a piece of hardwood so that it fits snugly within the grooves.

STEP 4 Slice strips from that piece of hardwood and screw them into place in the grooves of the lower deck.

STEP 5 The two upper decks may still be a bit tight when you slide them back and forth on the lower deck, so you may need to relieve the sides of the hardwood strips with a very sharp paring chisel as shown here. Continue this process, making frequent checks of the upper decks' tightness until you achieve the kind of fit you want: one that allows the decks to move freely but not sloppily.

STEP 6 Then, smooth the sidewalls of the grooves with a scrap of sandpaper.

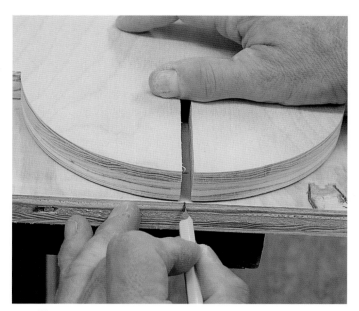

STEP 7 With the upper decks in position on the hardwood strips, mark the center of the notches that will enclose the machine screw used to lock one of the upper decks in place. Then, guided by your try square, make a line starting at that mark, a line along which you will place the hole for the wood-insert nut, into which you will turn the machine screw.

STEP 8 Drill the hole for the wood-insert nut on the drill press so the axis of the hole will be perpendicular to the surface of the deck.

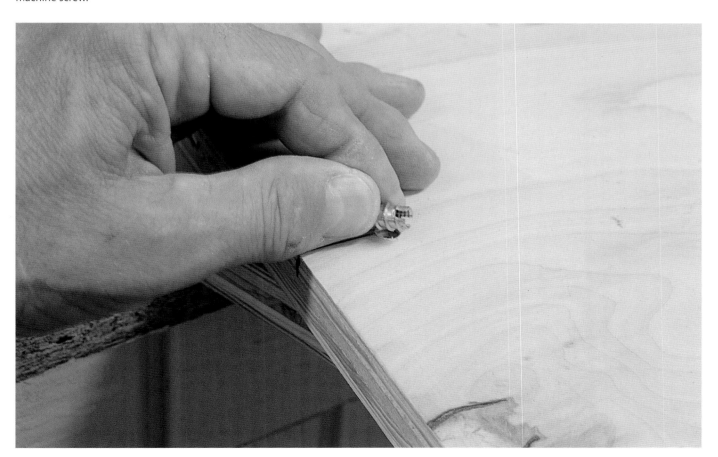

STEP 9 The wood-insert nut has coarse threads on its exterior surfaces which will engage the sidewalls of the hole. It also has fine threads on the interior surfaces to accept the machine screw.

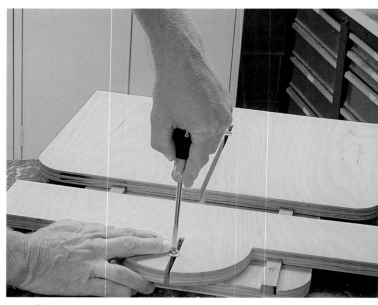

STEP 10 These nuts should be turned into their openings very carefully so they don't come apart under torque.

STEP 11 The machine screw and a washer make it possible to lock the upper deck into any required position. This flexibility is important because there is a great range of front and back chair ladder width. The front ladder of a no.7 production chair from the New Lebanon factory is 24" wide while the back ladder of one of the small Enfield chairs I build is only 15" wide.

STEP 12 After the upper decks have been fit to the lower deck, screw the fence in place.

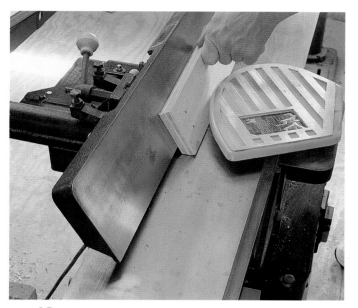

STEP 13 The two upper decks are raised on double thicknesses of plywood in order to make space available for the arching of the bent slats on the back ladders of the chairs I'll be mortising on this jig. To create even more space for this arching, relieve one corner of the top layer of plywood on both upper decks.

STEP 14 Then, glue and screw the plywood sandwich together.

STEP 15 Screw the lower deck to the angled deck supports.

STEP 16 In order to switch from cutting side-rung mortises on the back ladder to side-rung mortises on the front ladder, you need to be able to rotate the jig 180°. The jig achieves this rotation by turning on a bolt that protrudes from the wood table of the drill press up through a wood hinge leaf on the bottom of my SRMJ. When the upper decks are complete, make this wood hinge by fastening the leaves together with a door hinge.

STEP 17 Before you fasten the wood hinge to the bottom of your jig, check the placement of the hinge. It must be positioned so that the lower leaf sits flat on the table when the upper leaf is screwed to the bottom of the jig's lower deck.

STEP 18 The bolt on the left hand side of the photo will be installed with its head under the wood table I have bolted permanently to the metal table of my drill press. The shaft of the bolt will then pass through the metal sleeve in the lower leaf of the wood hinge. The nut will then be loosely turned onto the bolt holding the hinge — and therefore the entire jig — into position on the drill press table. Use a little epoxy to mount the sleeve in its hole.

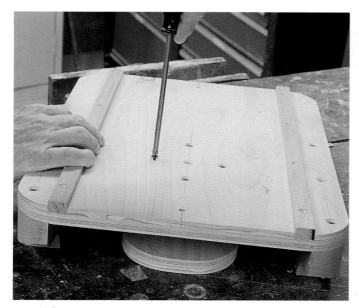

STEP 19 Then, screw the upper leaf of the wood hinge to the bottom of the lower deck as shown.

STEP 20 All of my drill press jigs are designed to be either bolted or clamped to this wood table which is itself bolted to the drill press' metal table. The bolt you see protruding up through the table is the bolt I discussed in the caption for step 16.

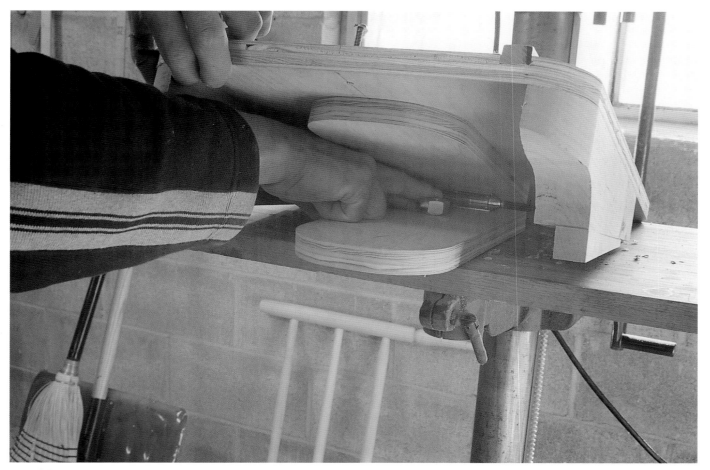

STEP 21 Mount the SRMJ by sliding the bottom leaf of the wood hinge over the bolt protruding up through the drill press table. Then, turn the nut onto that bolt "fingertight".

STEP 22 Place the fence deck on the lower deck, positioning it so the Forstner bit will drill a mortise into the middle of the front ladder's posts when those posts are crowded against the fence. Unfortunately, you can't measure from the fence to determine the fence placement on this deck because the angle at which the jig holds the fence confuses those measurements. Instead, I set the fence by eye and confirm my guess by holding a bit of scrap post against the fence and drilling a test mortise. If the mortise is in the center of the post, the jig is properly positioned. If the mortise is not in the center of the post, I move the fence and try again. This sounds more difficult than it is. After many years of using this jig, I find that I nail the center on my first guess nearly every time.

STEP 23 Position the other upper deck, placing it so that the front ladder's other post, the one not being mortised, lies on the deck's plywood sandwich.

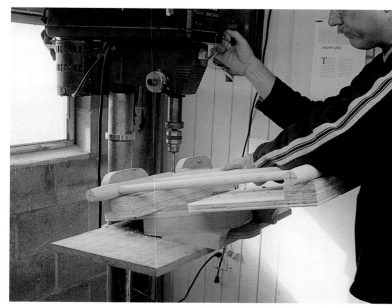

STEP 24 This is what the jig should look like when it's used to cut side-rung mortises in front ladders. To cut side-rung mortises in back ladders, the deck is rotated 180° on the bolt that holds it to the wood drill press table. The fences are then removed and repositioned so that the fence deck is below the business end of the drill press and the other deck supports the back post not being mortised.

STEP 25 This jig makes it possible to drill accurate side-rung mortises with ease.

STEP 26 This view of the deck in use shows how the bit engages the work.

CHAPTER SEVEN

Holding Devices

You can't do good hand-tool work unless the stock you're working is securely held in place. A woodworking vice is the most important holding device in any shop, but there are other shop-made holding and clamping devices that can make your woodworking life much more pleasurable and successful.

Bench Aides

If your workbench is equipped with holes for bench dogs, you can buy factory-made dogs to use in those holes, but you can also make your own dogs which you can configure to meet your personal specifications.

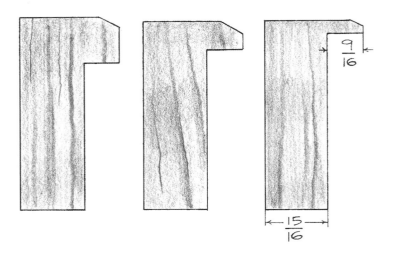

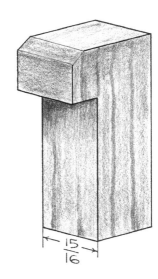

STEP 1 The two finished bench dogs are laying on a piece of cherry from which I'll cut three more bench dogs, following the drawings on the surface of that piece of cherry. The cherry has been planed so that its thickness is a bit less than the width of the bench-dog holes on my bench. Notice that two completed dogs and the three sketched dogs have heads of different heights. This is important because when I'm working panels of different thicknesses, I want dogs with heads of different heights so that the head is below the top surface of the panel I'm working.

STEP 2 Here are the completed dogs in operation used to help hold a round tabletop while I sand it. Notice the long, slender wedge of cherry I've tapped into place to hold that tabletop securely in place. The two wedges in the foreground can be used in a similar manner to hold other panels between a pair of bench dogs.

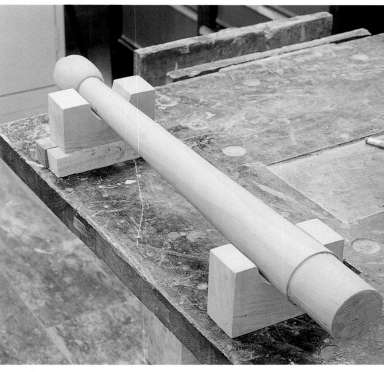

STEP 3 You can't work round, lathe-turned stock without U-blocks, and in my shop I have a deep drawer full of wedges, dogs and U-blocks from which I can pull bench aides of almost any size and shape.

STEP 4 This photo shows how U-blocks of two different sizes can be used to support a turned object with varying diameters.

STEP 5 When I'm using U-blocks to support turned stock, I pad the U-blocks with folded pieces of scrap cloth. I then clamp the object in place using the U-blocks.

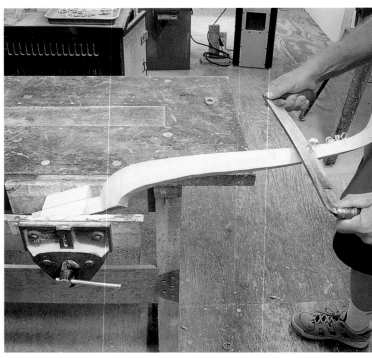

STEP **6** A third U-block will give you even greater holding power.

STEP **7** A pair of V-blocks can be used to hold a cabriole leg in your vise in a position that allows you to fair together two faces of the cabriole leg.

STEP **8** This detail shows how the V-blocks fit into the vise. Notice that in order to hold this rather thin leg post, I had to select V-blocks small enough so that the depth of the V cut in each is less than the thickness of the post being worked.

STEP 9 This is the finished Queen Anne table, the leg of which was being worked in steps 7 and 8.

PHOTO CREDIT: GARRY FRAZIER

Drawer Clamping Jig

Dovetailed drawer parts need to be brought together under the force of a set of clamps. If, instead, you try to bang things together with a mallet, particularly if the parts are tightly fit, something could break.

Human muscles aren't designed to exert the necessary pressure; therefore, most of us use pipe or bar clamps for such an application. The problem is that these clamps are loose and need to be held in position at the same time the screws are being turned in order to exert pressure on the joints being brought together. However, wood-workers only have two hands. To remedy this situation, I designed a very simple jig that allows me to work at this task in a more leisurely and organized manner.

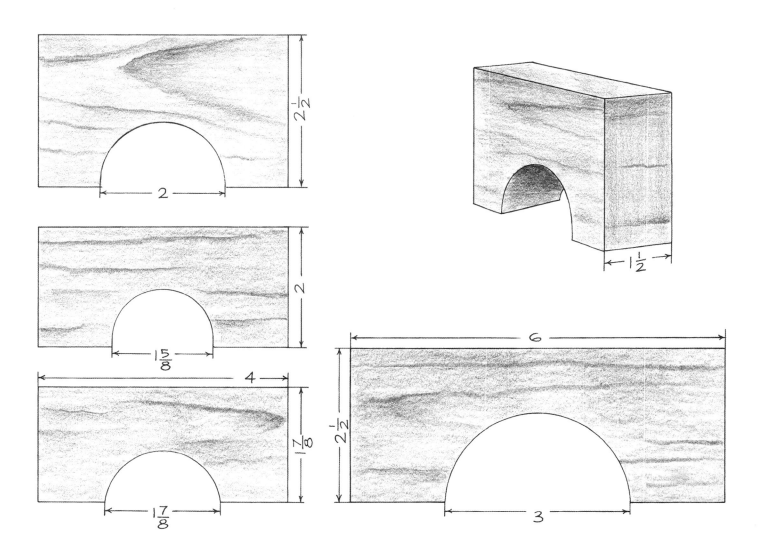

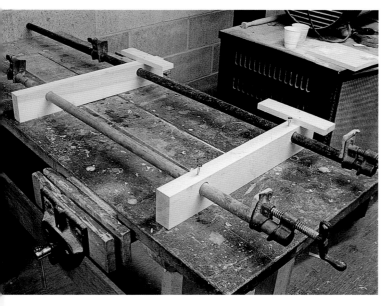

This is what the jig looks like before it's put to use. Notice that the two pipe clamps, which will be used on the bottoms of the drawer sides, are correctly spaced via the holes in the two lengths of thick maple. These holes have been drilled to the correct width for the set of drawers I'm about to assemble, in particular, a set of drawers for a Queen Anne highboy.

The little cleat nailed to the top surface near the back end of each of these lengths of maple is to compensate for the narrower width of the drawer back. A narrower width is necessary in order to allow the drawer bottom to be slid into its grooves.

This is the completed highboy, including the drawer being assembled in the previous photos.

PHOTO CREDIT: BRIAN KELLETT

Here is the jig in use. Notice that a little cleat has been attached to each end of each drawer side with a length of masking tape. That cleat is the surface against which the pipe clamps exert their pressure. The cleat is set so that it's positioned behind the dovetail pins that will be drawn into the gaps between the tails. Once the pipe clamps have fully seated the tails, I remove the clamps, square up the drawer and set it aside to dry.

WOOD STORAGE RACK
FRONT VIEW

$3\frac{1}{2}$

PORTABLE
PLANER

JOINTER

TABLE SAW

70

CHAPTER EIGHT

Shop Design

Woodworking shops tend to grow, weedlike, throughout whatever rooms and buildings we woodworkers have available. They can begin quite small, and then, in a surprisingly few years, take over every inch of space not otherwise claimed for living or recreation.

Typically, the first shop is a bench in the garage or in the basement, scattered with a handful of department store tools. In that rough environment, the unwitting craftsman is smitten with the urge to buy more tools and more materials, to make more and larger and more complex pieces. Then, as each new tool and each new load of materials enters the basement or the garage, more space must be allocated for woodworking.

The shop grows in this manner, in fits and starts, a bit at a time, as need and budget dictate.

A table saw is usually the first bench tool the craftsman purchases. This machine, even in its smaller sizes, is a space hog, requiring a significant amount of open air on both the infeed and outfeed ends, and on either side as well, particularly if the tool is going to be used to cut sheet goods. After all, a 4×8 sheet of plywood takes up a lot space.

Later the craftsman may purchase other machines: a radial arm saw or a cutoff saw, a jointer, a planer, a drill press, maybe a bandsaw and a lathe. As each new bench tool enters the shop, more space must be made available.

Concurrent with this acquisition of machinery, there is an inevitable accumulation of hand tools: saws, planes, scrapers, shaving tools, marking gauges and on and on. Although, individually, these tools don't take up much room, they do need to be stored somewhere, and that means tool chests or cabinets need to be added to the shop environment.

It's often at this time, after the accumulation of both bench and hand tools has begun in earnest, that the craftsman begins to think about either building a new shop from the ground up or, at the very least, remodeling an existing building so that it becomes a shop. In either case, the craftsman sets out with the idea of creating a building specifically configured to suit the kind of woodworking the craftsman intends to practice.

My very first shop was the hitch of the 28-foot travel trailer my wife and I lived in shortly after our marriage. When I wanted to saw a board to length, I either laid it across the hitch or held it in a vice I had clamped to the hitch. I then worked the cut material in my lap, inside the travel trailer, making small sculptures and a chess set.

My second shop was the extra bedroom in the mobile home we purchased to replace our travel trailer: an extra bedroom which I had to surrender after the arrival of our daughter Emily. That room measured less than ten feet on a side, but working in that cramped environment, I nevertheless managed to turn out several pieces of full-sized furniture, including a chest of drawers and an enormous aquarium built of birch plywood and lined with fiberglass and resin.

Once, during our stay in that mobile home, when my wife flew home to spend a week with her parents, I used the living room as a shop. I pushed the furniture aside, set up my table saw and jointer, and over the period of that one week transformed a load of birch into a six-foot tall china cabinet. Then a couple of hours before I left for the airport to pick up my wife, I frantically vacuumed every bit of evidence from the carpet, the draperies and the furniture. To this day, she has no knowledge of this woodworking indiscretion. She believes I built the china cabinet in our extra bedroom.

When my daughter Emily crowded me out of that extra bedroom (and I was glad to be crowded out for so worthy a purpose), I built my first actual shop, a frame building measuring 14x16, part of which I partitioned off so that my wife could have a potting shed. That first actual shop was also small, but it was, nevertheless, an enormous improvement on any working space I had ever before owned. I placed my table saw — a stamped metal table with a handheld circular saw clamped underneath — just inside the shop door. This allowed me to rip material that was a bit more than eight feet in length with the shop door open, although when I cut up sheet goods, I had to take the table saw out into the yard. I set up my radial arm saw — my first real bench tool — along one wall with a four-foot-long bench on the infeed side. I next purchased a 4⅛" jointer which I located beside the table saw.

Then over 20 years ago, when my wife and I moved to Ohio, we purchased our first real house. During our search for real estate, my wife focused her attention on the houses themselves, while I concentrated on any outbuildings that

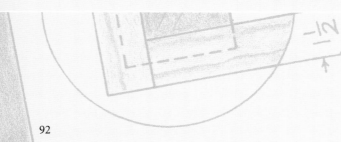

could be made into shops without too much effort and expense. The house we chose, the house in which we still live, met most of our requirements. First, it was beautifully situated in the middle of a 2 acre wooded lot (which I noticed included a number of cherry and walnut trees large enough to be harvested). And it had two buildings. One was a semi-attached garage measuring 14×24, which became my first shop at this address. The other was a two-story concrete-block building measuring 24×24. After I had replaced some rotten rafters and put on a new roof, after I sprayed for powder post beetles and replaced some honey-combed floorboards, after I partitioned off a room small enough to be heated with a woodburner, I moved my tools into this larger building and began constructing furniture in earnest.

For almost 20 years, I worked in that shop without making any real improvements to my working space. The reason was simple: I didn't have time. I couldn't make both furniture and a shop; however, when the opportunity to write this book came along, I realized it was my chance finally to get my woodworking life in order.

I knew that my first objective was to gain the upper hand in my decades-long battle with scrap. Chair-making constitutes most of the woodworking that takes place in my shop, and because the material for chair parts must be perfect through and through, I had a lot of rips and cutoffs that were too nice — at least on one side — to throw away.

And so it accumulated, month after month, year after year, taking up more and more space in my shop until it became hard to work and even harder to do the photography required by my magazine and book assignments.

As a result, when I began to fantasize about my shop remodel, my fantasies initially focused on an enormous rack on which I would stack both unused material and scrap.

The shop remodel I eventually settled upon reflects the five principles of shop layout that I've come to accept after 30 years as a furniture maker:

1. Every productive shop must devote a substantial percentage of its floor space to scrap management.

2. Good lighting is essential. It isn't possible to do effective sanding and finishing in uncertain light. (Bright reflective ceilings and walls make good lighting even more effective.)

3. The table saw and jointer, two tools at the heart of most woodworking shops, should be positioned side by side for two reasons. First, in most cases, freshly ripped edges needed to be smoothed and flattened on the jointer. The jointer, therefore, should be positioned close to the table saw for economy of movement. Second, these are the two machines over which long stock will most often pass. Positioning them side by side allows you to make the best possible use of the same long corridor of space.

4. The radial arm saw needs long infeed and outfeed tables, even if the saw is never used to rip material. Long tables make the process of cutting long stock to length much less troublesome.

5. The planer is the most prolific manufacturer of dust and chips in many shops. For that reason, I have equipped mine with wheels that allow me to roll it up to the open overhead door of my wood storage room where it can eject this dirt into the driveway.

Shop Drawings

The following drawings represent the shops of five craftsmen who have worked at furniture making long enough to give serious thought to shop design. One, Mark Rasche, of New Albany, Ohio has been a full-time professional woodworker for 20 years. Others, Bob Konesni, of Toledo, Ohio for example, are advanced amateurs who use their shop environments to create furniture for their own personal use, as well as for the use of friends and family.

THE ONE-MAN SHOP
Mark Rasche

Although Rasche has had employees for most of the 18 years he's been in business just outside of New Albany, Ohio, there are times when he has to work alone. To help him accomplish this, he built three shop carts and created a shop-floor plan that make it possible for a single man to move materials — even 4×8 sheets of plywood — from machine to machine with little physical effort.

The floor plan of Rasche's shop is designed around four principles. First, his Unisaw is embedded in a table large enough to support full sheets of plywood as they're being fed past the blade. Second, the Unisaw, as well as his shaper and edger, is equipped with a stock feeder that reduces operator fatigue. Third, there is enough space on both the infeed and outfeed ends of each machine for cart placement. This permits a single operator to pull a board from one cart, feed it into the machine, then pull it off the machine at the other end and place it on a second cart. And last, machinery and benches are placed so that there is a wide enough aisle between each to permit the easy passage of the stock carts.

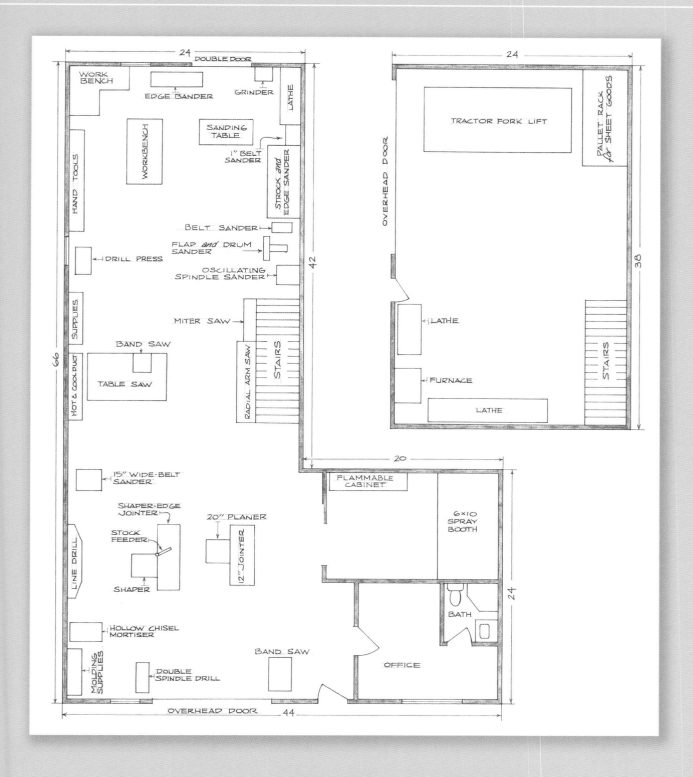

95

A CABINETMAKER'S SHOP

Jim Pierce

When you enter my dad's shop in Fostoria, Ohio, you are struck by its cramped interior, this despite the fact that the room measures 24' in length and 14' in width, an interior some woodworkers would regard as spacious.

There are two reasons for the claustrophobic atmosphere in his shop. First, 4' of the room's length are taken up by a stickered wood pile on one end and an additional 3' of its length are taken up by a wood rack on the other end, effectively reducing the length of the room from 24' to 17'. In addition, he has eight bench tools, each of which has a fairly sizable footprint.

This crowded interior means that he must plan his shop operations carefully. For example, if he is building a cabinet with a number of machine-cut mortises, he must make sure that he gets all of his mortises cut at the same time because to get at the drill press he uses for mortising, he must slide his shaper to one side and drag the drill press toward the center of the shop in order to have the necessary elbow room. If he forgets a single mortise, he has to once again slide his machinery around in order to free up the drill press for that single mortise.

His shop is laid out with his jointer and table saw in the center so that he can use the same long corridor of space for handling long material as it is worked back and forth between these two tools. He places his shaper between the table saw and jointer to also make use of this space.

To facilitate cutting large pieces of sheet stock in his cramped shop, he built his workbench so that its top is several inches lower than the deck of his table saw, thus preventing collisions with the bench top when he is feeding sheet goods past the table saw blade.

He is content with very modest infeed and outfeed tables for his radial-arm saw, although he does try to keep clear the areas to the right and left of this machine so that he can, if necessary, cut long stock here.

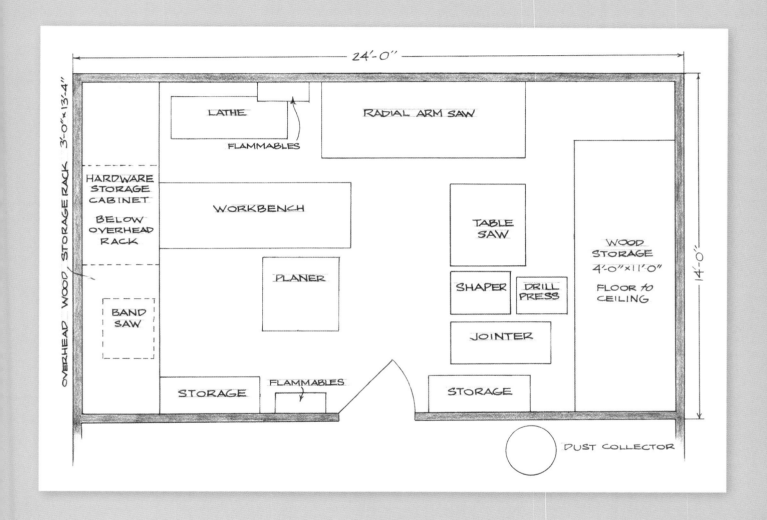

A MULTI-PURPOSE SHOP

Bob Konesni

Bob Konesni of Toledo, Ohio, designed his shop around a large open area which serves several functions. First, it gives him the space he needs to cut up 4×8 sheet goods. Second, it provides him with a staging area for large material deliveries. And third, since he uses his shop for metalwork as well as woodwork, it provides Konesni with a large open area that can be easily swept clean so that welding doesn't have an opportunity to ignite piles of sawdust. In addition, this same space is sometimes used as a finishing area.

The large table on the outfeed end of the table saw also serves more than one purpose. It supports long stock as it comes off the table saw. It also serves as a large, open area in which Konesni can layout and glueup furniture assemblies.

He located his horizontal mortising machine near his lathe so that, when he's creating table legs, he can move quickly from turning to mortising.

The side-by-side placement of his radial-arm saw and his compound miter saw may appear to be an exercise in redundancy, but Konesni's thinking here is sound. This placement allows him to use the same long tables for both tools, and he needs both because the radial-arm saw, while perfectly suited for 90° cuts, is less suited to angle cuts which Konesni performs with his compound miter saw.

Finally, Konesni has done what many of us do with his primary bench: He has positioned it in front of the window which offers the best view of the world outside.

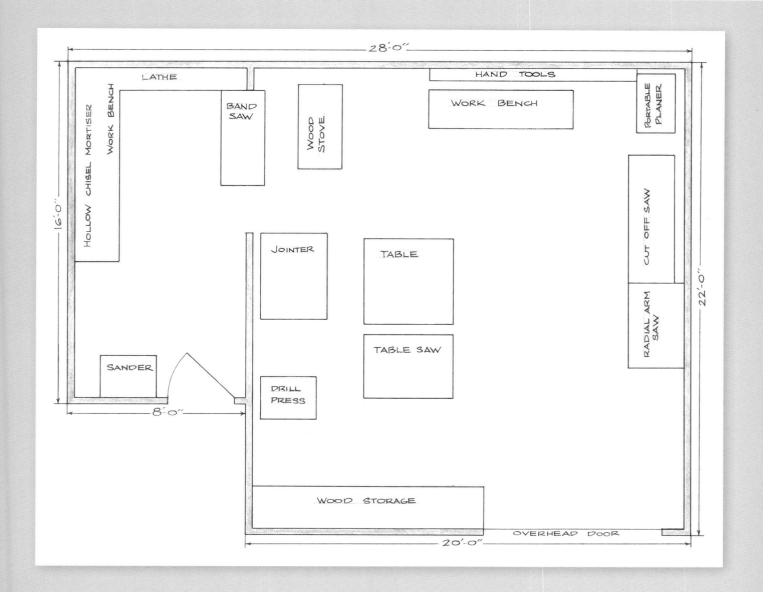

SHOP ON WHEELS

Ed Moser

There's never enough room in the shop. This is true for the craftsman working in a 100 square-foot corner of his garage. It's also true for the craftsman working in 40,000 square-feet of rented space in an industrial park.

Some craftsmen address the need for space by cleverly fitting one machine set-up into another, as Bob Konesni did with his radial-arm saw and compound miter saw. But Ed Moser of Bowling Green, Ohio, has a different approach.

Ed has mounted all of his bench tools, as well as his workbench, on wheels so that pieces not currently in use can be easily moved aside. For example, if he's cutting sheet goods on his table saw, he pushes the table saw into the center of the room and rolls his work-bench into position to use it as an outfeed table. As Moser points out, this approach "requires a little advance planning," but it does make it possible for someone working in a small space to tackle large projects.

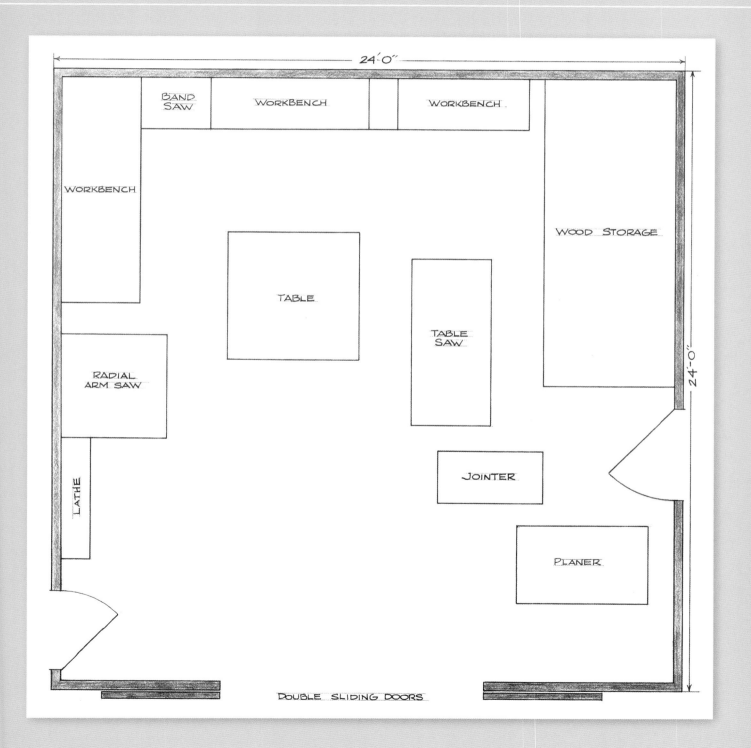

24'-0"

BAND SAW

WORKBENCH

WORKBENCH

WORKBENCH

WOOD STORAGE

TABLE

TABLE SAW

RADIAL ARM SAW

LATHE

JOINTER

PLANER

24'-0"

DOUBLE SLIDING DOORS

A CHAIRMAKER'S SHOP

Kerry Pierce

Approximately 60-70% of my business is chairmaking, so my shop is designed to help me accomplish that goal as quickly and efficiently as possible.

When rough material comes in my shop door, it typically goes first to the radial arm saw where it is chopped to approximate length. Incoming material is often 6 to10 feet in length so I need fairly long infeed and outfeed tables on that saw, this despite the fact that the saw is never used for ripping. And because my post stock is sometimes 3" thick and 10-12" wide, these tables need to be pretty beefy. To meet these needs, I constructed the table frames from 2 × 4 lumber which I lag-screwed to the wall of my shop. I also made the tables long enough so that — together with the actual radial-arm saw table — I have nearly ten feet of bench length on which I can lay the material I'm cutting.

To take further advantage of this long bench space, I fit my router table into the infeed side of the radial arm saw table, allowing me to use this long bench for this purpose as well. By placing the router table so that its business end is well forward of the radial arm saw fence, I can set up most router applications without having to remove the radial arm saw fence.

Material next moves to my jointer where it is straightened before ripping. Because I often work back and forth between this machine and my table saw, I positioned the two machines side by side. This arrangement offers one additional benefit. On those occasions when I am working with long stock, placing the table saw and jointer side by side allows me to use the same long corridor of space for both machines.

My thickness planer is my most prolific dust generator. For that reason, I keep it in my wood room, rather than in the shop itself. When I run the planer, I push it (it's mounted on a wheeled table) to the open overhead door, where it ejects its Amazonian stream of chips into the driveway. I then periodically shovel up the chips and cart them to the burn pile. In this way, I prevent the planer from clogging the hoses on my shop vacuum, as well as the air I breathe.

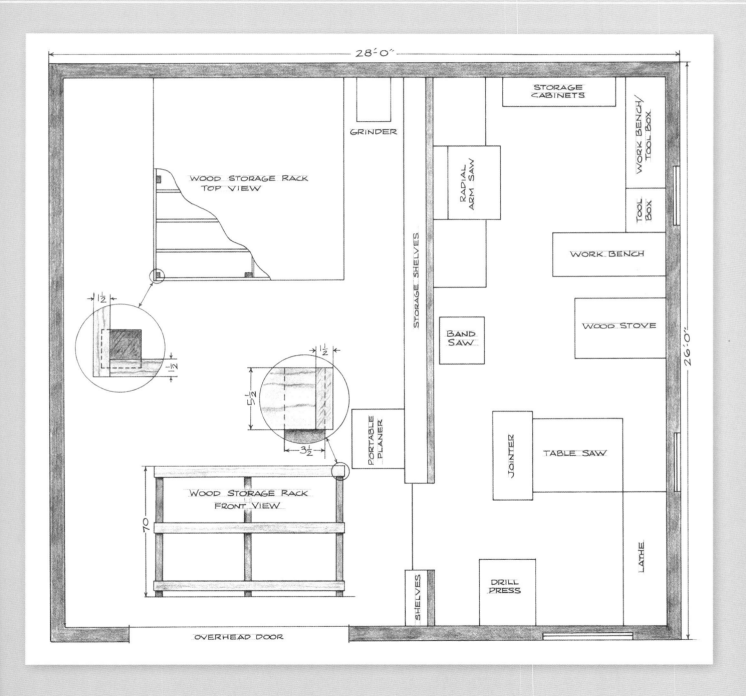

28'-0"

GRINDER

STORAGE CABINETS

WORK BENCH / TOOL BOX

WOOD STORAGE RACK TOP VIEW

RADIAL ARM SAW

TOOL BOX

$1\frac{1}{2}$

STORAGE SHELVES

WORK BENCH

$\frac{1}{2}$

BAND SAW

WOOD STOVE

26'-0"

$1\frac{1}{2}$

$5\frac{1}{2}$

PORTABLE PLANER

JOINTER

TABLE SAW

$3\frac{1}{2}$

WOOD STORAGE RACK FRONT VIEW

70

LATHE

SHELVES

DRILL PRESS

OVERHEAD DOOR

KERRY PIERCE

PHOTO AT LEFT The white walls and ceiling of my newly remodeled bench room provide a bright area in which to work. This view reveals the storage cabinets I installed under the infeed and outfeed tables of my radial arm saw.

Please notice also the router table mounted in the infeed table of my radial arm saw. Because I mounted my router in a position that puts the business end well forward of the radial arm saw table fence, I can perform most routing tasks without removing the radial arm saw fence.

PHOTO AT RIGHT I have a pair of machinists cabinets in which I keep most of my hand tools. The cabinet immediately behind my bench has a top compartment in which I keep most of my chisels and gouges. The drawer below that is reserved for screwdrivers. The top drawer of the unit behind that cabinet is filled with various type of pliers, channel-locks and Vise-Grips. The second drawer of that back cabinet is chock-full of files and rasps. The drawers below are reserved for other similar groupings of tools. This organization of hand tools is an important time saver because it enables me to quickly put my hands on any hand tool I might need. And at the end of every work day, no matter how tired I may be, I force myself to put every tool in its drawer.

PHOTO ABOVE When the weather is warm, I use my wood room as a finishing area. In this photo, a trio of Shaker tripod tables are drying after receiving a second coat of Waterlox. My planer cabinet on wheels sits behind the drying tables. When I need to thickness material, I roll the cabinet to the open overhead door of my wood room and eject chips into the driveway. As part of my shop remodel, I installed over 70 lineal feet of shelving on the wall behind my planer. By itself, that installation significantly improved my ability to function efficiently in my shop.

PHOTO ABOVE I have always loved the time I spend in my shop, but now that my shop remodel has improved my working environment so significantly, I take even greater pleasure in the hours I spend there. And that, of course, is what this woodworking business is all about: the shameless pursuit of pleasure.

PHOTO AT LEFT This wood rack has enabled me to gain the upper hand in my thirty-year battle with scrap. The top deck — closest to the ceiling and, as a result, the warmest in the summer months — is where I finish dry lumber after bringing it inside. The bottom rack is where I store dry lumber, and the middle deck, which I sheathed with 5/8 plywood is where I keep all the oddments of scrap which are too nice to load into my wood burner but too small for most project applications.

JIM PIERCE

PHOTO ABOVE My dad's cluttered shop would be problematic for many craftsmen, but Dad has never felt any great need to establish order in the chaos that has evolved there. In fact, it's his contention that — in a matter of moments — he can lay his hand on any specific bit of wood in his shop, even a piece he cut five or ten years in the past.

I don't doubt this. I've seen him prove it often enough, but I also know I couldn't be comfortable working in such a setting.

PHOTO AT LEFT My dad's packrat nature has paid many dividends. This hutch, for example, is made entirely of walnut pallet wood he salvaged and stored for many years in his cluttered shop.

MARK RASCHE

Mark Rasche, of New Albany, Ohio, maintains one of the neatest and best equipped one-man shops I have ever been in. Here, he stands in front of a patternmaker's lathe he bought used and moved into his shop.

Rasche maintains a small office just inside the front door of his shop. This office, like his shop, is enviably clean and well ordered.

BOB KONESNI

PHOTO AT LEFT In Bob Konesni's Toledo, Ohio shop the same long surfaces are used to support stock being cut on the compound miter saw and the radial-arm saw.

PHOTO AT RIGHT Konesni's hand tool collection includes a number of antique woodworking planes.

ED MOSER

Ed Moser operates a part-time cabinetmaking business out of his Bowling Green, Ohio shop.

Moser's shop is housed in this attractive frame building behind his home.

CHAPTER NINE

Shop Tips

My earliest woodworking memory took place in a very dark workshop, a basement I think. My dad, then in his twenties, was helping me build a birdhouse. Or more accurately, I'm sure, I was helping him build a birdhouse for which he would later allow me to claim credit. I remember using my first real tool, a new Stanley block plane, one of those impossible-to-adjust 1950s confections painted a shockingly brilliant blue and red. I doubt very much if I managed to persuade that entry-level Stanley to so much as scuff up the birdhouse material, let alone remove a meaningful shaving.

But I remember gripping the plane in my pale hands. I remember pushing it along the edge of a board, my tongue clamped in the corner of my mouth just like my dad. And I remember a growing excitement as I witnessed the magical transformation of a pile of wood scraps into a house with four walls, a floor, a roof, and a little round door just large enough for a sparrow.

I've never lost my taste for that growing excitement, that strangely addictive growing excitement. In fact I had my most recent fix just this afternoon as I witnessed the magical transformation of a pile of wood scraps into a series of Shaker oval boxes and carriers.

There is magic in the transformation. Raw material is invested with purpose in a way I don't fully understand despite the fact that I've witnessed it a thousand times in the last half century. Veneer becomes box sides. Quarter-inch white pine becomes lids and bottoms. There is magic in the transformation, but there is also technique.

Fifty years of experience and experiment have filled my head with technique, much of it unavailable to me until I pick up material and begin to work. As I prepared this book, I kept a notebook in my shop, and whenever I remembered something I'd done that had helped me produce useful results, I scribbled a note. The tips that follow are the result of those notes.

SHOP TIP 1 Flipping Pieces Being Ripped

When you're ripping long stock, you can push the work past the blade with push sticks, like those I describe in Chapter 3. You can also flip the stock after you've ripped it halfway along its length. This method is even safer than using push sticks.

SHOP TIP 2 Centering Turning Stock on the Bandsaw

If your band saw has a notch on the infeed side of the blade to allow you to install new blades, you can use your band saw to quickly and accurately center stock for turning.

Lay one corner of the square turning blank in the notch. Then, press the blank against the running blade, holding it so that the corner opposite the one in the notch is bisected by the blade. This will result in a saw cut that connects the bottom corner with the top corner with a clearly drawn diagonal. The saw kerfs also give you locations on the end grain in which you can press the drive spurs of your lathe center. After you've marked your centers, you can then use one of the saw cradles discussed in Chapter 5 to create octagons.

SHOP TIP 3 Drill Press Table

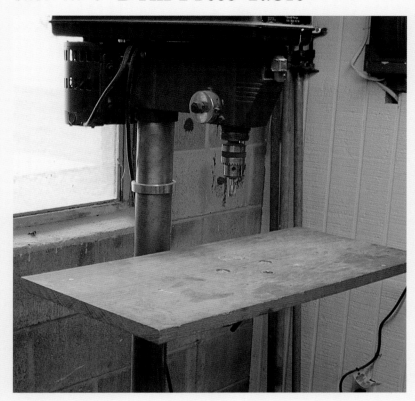

I've never been happy with the tiny tables that come with most drill presses. Despite the fact that I believe most people who buy drill presses do so with the intention of using the machine in a wood-shop, the tables are configured to be used in a machine shop. To remedy this, I added a bolt-on wood table that gives me a large, flat surface on which I can mount any of the drill press jigs I use. The table also gives me a surface on which I can lay fairly large wood parts while I work with them on the drill press.

SHOP TIP 4 Installing Solid Wood Drawer Bottoms

Drawer bottoms on full-sized period furniture can be very wide. If the drawer bottom is made of plywood, this wide construction will shrink only a negligible amount across that width, but if the drawer bottom is made of solid wood, like the cherry example shown here, the panel will shrink appreciably across its width. The drawer bottom shown here might shrink as much as a quarter inch.

If the drawer bottom is held in position by a nail or a screw, turned in through a hole in the drawer bottom into the bottom edge of the draw-er back, that shrinkage will almost certainly draw the front edge of the drawer bottom from its groove on the back side of the drawer front. The little notch shown here, through which the mounting screw is being turned, allows you to make a correction if drawer bottom shrinkage pulls the front of the drawer bottom from its groove. Simply loosen the screw, reposition the drawer bottom, and retighten the screw.

113

Squaring Up Dovetailed Cases

The upper case of the highboy shown at right is held together by a set of fat dovetails at each corner. Despite all the joinery, it is possible for the newly glued case to be out of square. To determine the squareness of the case, measure the diagonals. If the case is square (and the two sides are the same length and the top and bottom are the same length), the diagonal measurements will be identical.

If the diagonals are not the same length, you can rack the case into square by pressing one corner of the longer diagonal against a firm surface as I'm doing here. Repeat until the diagonals are the same. When the diagonals are the same length, the case is square.

The case being racked in the previous photo is the upper case of this highboy.

PHOTO CREDIT: BRIAN KELLETT

SHOP TIP 6 Creating Moldings with a Gauge Block

The highboy shown on the previous page has a wide moulding which conceals a secret drawer. The moulding was created with hand planes. The little gauge block shown here allowed me to assess the moulding shape at various locations along its length.

SHOP TIP 7 Creating Mortises with a Gauge Block

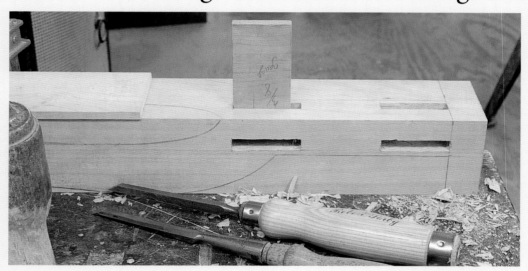

When you're chopping mortises by hand, a gauge block, like the one shown here, can simplify the process.

SHOP TIP 8 Gluing Preparation

A gluing session should begin only after preparation. This preparation should include a parts inventory to ensure that all necessary parts are where they should be. In this photo, I have started my preparation for a gluing session by laying out the parts I'll be gluing together.

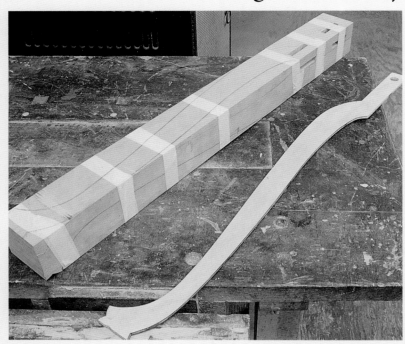

Complicated shapes, like a cabriole leg, can be created by band-sawing stock in two adjacent planes. The cabriole leg blank has been taped back together after being bandsawn in one plane. The blank will then be rotated 90° and bandsawn in the adjacent plane.

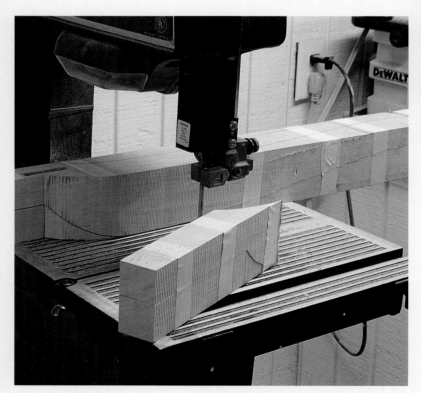

The cabriole leg shown in the preceding photos was used in the construction of this little Queen Anne table.

The leg blank from the previous photo has been partially sawn in the adjacent plane. These rips should be re-attached with masking tape to stabilize the blank during the remaining sawing.

Flattening Glued-Up Panels

Any craftsman who does a lot of case-work often finds himself leveling glued-up panels too wide for his jointer to flatten and his planer to thickness. This work can be done the old-fashioned way using hand planes. The plane to start with in such a situation is a scrub plane with a cambered iron, like the one shown here on the right. This iron will quickly level glued-up panels.

A scrub plane with a cambered iron leaves behind a rippled surface like the one shown here. The ripples can be taken out with a Stanley no.80 (one of my favorite tools), followed by a smoothing plane.

Giving Up Sub-Assemblies

Gluing-up sub-assemblies is critical work. A mistake here can ruin parts that might have taken many hours to fabricate. Before I begin such a process, I take a few moments to figure out how I'm going to do what needs to be done. In this photo, I'm gluing up a pair of end panels for a Queen Anne table. Notice that I raised the actual panel on a piece of scrap so I could work the legs onto the tenons in the end panels without interference from the bench top. This simple device made it possible to work quickly and efficiently through the gluing-up process.

In this photo, I'm gluing up the entire table frame by bringing together the end panels from the previous photo with the two side panels. Again, I've raised the work on scrap, this time so the arch in the cabriole legs clears the bench top.

Making Stands for Planers and Drum Sanders

My thickness planer and my drum sander are on wheels so I can push them to the overhead door of my wood room so that the dust and chips they generate can be ejected onto the driveway outside. Both machines are bolted to simple cubes sheathed in 5/8" plywood. These cubes are constructed around 2x4 frames. To build the frames, I started by spiking together four corner posts for each cube. I then attached the horizontal parts of the frames using metal corner brackets. I did this because I didn't want to take the time to create elegant joinery for these strictly utilitarian stands. In this photo, I'm attaching the metal corner brackets.

The wheels are attached to 2x4 blocks I spiked inside each corner of each cube.

The strength in these cubes comes, not from strong frame joinery but from a skin of 5/8 exterior plywood fastened to all four sides and the top of each cube. This plywood is attached with $1\frac{5}{8}$" drywall screws. In the foreground, I'm attaching the plywood top for the cube that will hold my drum sander. Behind me, painted white, you can see the cube I built for my Makita thickness planer.

A Drill-Powered Assist for Post Bending

It's very difficult to muscle a pair of 1⅜" diameter chair posts into a bending form, at least when you're relying on human muscle alone. You can achieve the same result however, with much less effort, by using a hose clamp and a screwdriver bit in your electric drill. This is most easily done with a drill-bit extension, like the one I'm using here. Without the extension, the business end of the drill will scuff itself against the clamp as it turns the screw.

This close-up shows the protective collars that keep the hose clamp from damaging the chair posts.

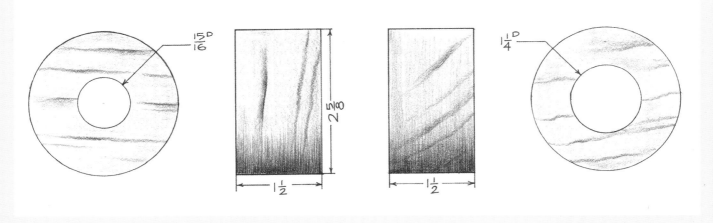

Illustration of the protective collars for the chair posts.

SHOP TIP 14 Shop-Made Hardware for Shop Cabinets

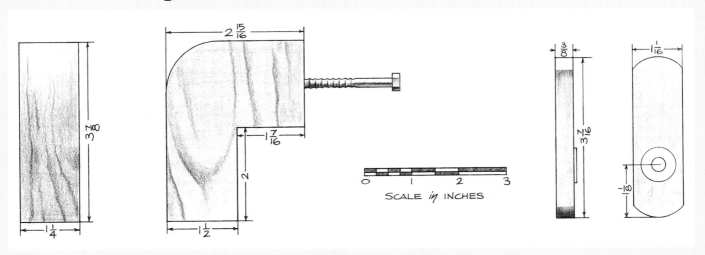

When you build shop cabinets out of exterior plywood fastened to a 2x4 shell — as I did in my shop — you'll find that it's difficult to tame the natural inclination of exterior plywood to exhibit twist, particularly if you're using that plywood, un-supported by a frame, for cabinet doors. To control that inclination, you need some really sturdy hardware. I recommend these two shop-made catches. The one shaped like an "L" from the side is designed to be screwed to the inside of the cabinet door with the "L" turning onto the 2x4 door frame. This catch holds one of a pair of doors tight against that frame.

This flat catch is then fastened, using a screw, to the outside of the door held with the "L" catch. The second door in the pair is held fast by rotating this flat catch until it traps the front of the second door in the pair of doors.

The cabinets on which I use these two catches can be seen in the first photo in the series documenting my shop.

Ripping on the Band Saw

Although it's possible to rip really thick stock on a table saw (by ripping the stock halfway through, flipping it over and passing it over the blade a second time), this work is done much more efficiently on the bandsaw. For one thing, the bandsaw is likely to be much faster than a table saw when used for that purpose, unless, of course, your table saw has one of those oversized 5hp motors the rest of us dream about. For another, there is the issue of cleanliness. Because the kerf cut by a table saw is much wider than the kerf cut by a bandsaw, the table saw creates more dust when plowing that kerf, dust which is then ejected into the air of the shop.

Matching Up Your Stock

When you're matching stock for a particular application (here I'm matching up some curly cherry for drawer fronts on a Queen Anne highboy), line the stock up along one wall and wet the stock down with a wash of water. (The water will reveal the color and figure the stock will exhibit after finishing.) Then mix and match the boards until you get the desired results.

SHOP TIP 17 Choosing the Best Part of the Best Piece

When we look at a board, we typically imagine any narrower width cut from that board as being parallel to one or the other of the board's sides. We typically think joint, then rip. However, we can often make better use of the material if we see that initial edge in a different way. Don't begin by straightening one of the board's existing edges. Instead, sketch in the edge that would make best use of the board's figure (as shown here). Then, with a straight-edge, delineate the board's initial edge, cut it on your bandsaw, then pass it over your jointer. The parallel cut on the other side of the board can be made on your table saw.

SHOP TIP 18 Jointing Wide Stock

Sometimes it's necessary to work with material that's too wide to be flattened on the 6" jointer so many of us have in our shops. If you find yourself in that predicament, there are two possible solutions. One is to work one side of the board with a scrub plane and a pair of winding sticks. Then feed the material to your 12" planer. This is the classical solution to the problem, but there is another, easier option you might consider.

First, rip the board in half, even if that cut makes the material too narrow for its intended use. Then flatten each of the halves on your jointer and reassemble the two flattened halves with a glue joint. The resulting joint will result in a very slight visual discontinuity, one only the most eagle-eyed can spot.

Creating Wide Panels

Two hundred years ago, a furniture maker could find cherry and maple, and walnut boards that were 20" to 24" in width. Unfortunately, such boards are almost never seen anymore. This means that anyone doing casework must sometimes glue up wide panels from narrower boards.

If you're using pipe clamps for this task, it's important to raise the panel so that it is in line with the pressure points of the clamp head and tail stock. I use a pair of 1½" x 1½" cleats placed on either side of my pipe clamps for this purpose. The cleats do one other thing as well. They align the boards I'm joining so that their top surfaces and their bottom surfaces lay in the same planes.

Creating Wide Panels from Thin Stock

If you've tried using pipe clamps to join thin panels, you have almost certainly experienced buckling of the panel under the pressure of the clamps. This occurs because the boards from which you're gluing the panel have only thin edges making contact and any misalignment of these thin edges, however slight, will cause the panel to buckle.

A gentler alternative to pipe clamps, one that doesn't put so much pressure on the joints that the boards begin to buckle, requires the use of two pairs of wedges to apply pressure. First clamp two strips of one-inch thick material to the top of your bench. Place these strips so that they are a distance apart that is a little greater than the width of the panel you're about to glue. Then after applying glue to the jointed edges and positioning the boards from which you'll create the panel, position the pairs of wedges in the gap between the edge of the panel and one of the inch-thick strips you clamped to your bench top. Then tap the wedges together until their functional width increases enough to exert sufficient pressure on the joint to cause a bit of glue squeeze-out.

SHOP TIP 21 Fitting Drawers

When you're fitting drawers that will slide against the side of the case, you can reduce fitting problems by making the drawers a half inch too narrow, then applying a $\frac{1}{4}$" thick fitting strip to each side of the drawer. Then, when fitting the drawer to the case, it's necessary to plane only the strip, not the entire width of the drawer side. This method also reduces the amount of friction the drawer experiences when it's opened and closed.

SUPPLIERS

B&Q
B&Q Head Office
Portswood House
1 Hampshire Corporate Park
Chandler Ford
Eastleigh
Hampshire
SO53 3YX
0870 0101 006
www.diy.com
Tools, paint, wood, electrical, garden

BRIMARC ASSOCIATES
7/9 Ladbroke Park
Millers Road
Warwick
CV34 5AE
0845 330 9100
www.brimarc.com
Woodworking tools and accessories

THE HOME DEPOT
2455 Paces Ferry Road
Atlanta, Georgia 30339
800-553-3199 (U.S.)
800-668-2266 (Canada)
www.homedepot.com
Tools, paint, wood, electrical, garden

LEE VALLEY TOOLS LTD.
U.S.:
P.O. Box 1780
Ogdensburg, New York 13669-6780
800-267-8735
Canada:
P.O. Box 6295, Station J
Ottawa, Ontario, Canada K2A 1T4
800-267-8761
www.leevalley.com
Fine woodworking tools and hardware

LOWE'S HOME IMPROVEMENT WAREHOUSE
P.O. Box 1111
North Wilkesboro, North Carolina 28656
800-445-6937
www.lowes.com
Tools, paint, wood, electrical, garden

ROCKLER WOODWORKING AND HARDWARE
4365 Willow Drive
Medina, Minnesota 55340
800-279-4441
www.rockler.com
Woodworking tools and hardware

TOOL STATION
18 Whiteladies Road
Clifton
Bristol
BS8 2LG
0808 100 7211
www.toolstation.com
Power tools

WOODCRAFT
P.O. Box 1686
Parkersburg, West Virginia 26102-1686
800-225-1153
www.woodcraft.com
Woodworking hardware and accessories

INDEX

More Great Books from Popular Woodworking Books!

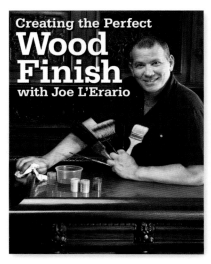

Master the three R's of wood finishing—restore, revive or remove—without worry or mistake. Nationally known woodworker Joe L'Erario offers easy-to-master tips, tricks and step-by-step instructions for applying flawless finishes every time. Includes full-color photos.

ISBN 1-55870-744-1, paperback, 128 pages, #70697-K

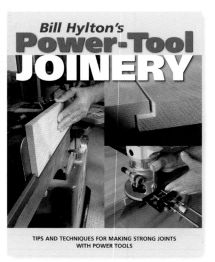

Use your power tools to cut a variety of strong, practical joints in no time at all! Learn how to select, cut and assemble a spectrum of joints including dadoes, grooves, splined and biscuit joints, rabbets, sliding dovetails, and more! Includes step-by-step color photos.

ISBN 1-55870-738-7, paperback, 128 pages, #70691-K

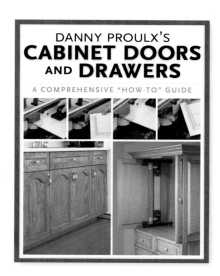

Woodworkers of all levels can master the tricky art of building and fitting doors and drawers with this full-color instruction book by master woodworker Danny Proulx. This how-to guide features step-by-step instructions for a variety of styles and techniques, concise directions for fitting and installing your project, and advice for choosing the best hardware for your project.

ISBN 1-55870-739-5, paperback, 128 pages, #70692-K

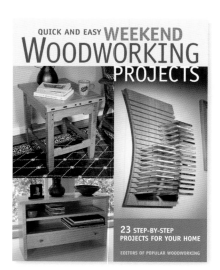

The editors of *Popular Woodworking* magazine show you how to build 23 sturdy, stylish projects all in one weekend! Efficient use of time and set up allows you to start your project on Friday and finish up by Sunday dinner! Includes full-color photos.

ISBN 1-55870-746-8, paperback, 128 pages, #70698-K

These and other great woodworking books are available at your local bookstore, woodworking stores, online suppliers or by calling 1-800-448-0915.